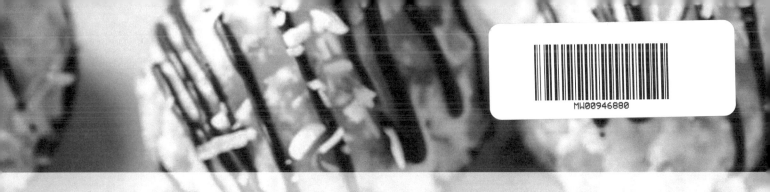

The Complete Ninja Flip
Air Fryer Cookbook

Delicious, Quick & Affordable Recipes to Air fry, Roast, Broil, Bake, Pizza, Dehydrate and More for Your Family | Save Counter Space

(Color Edition)

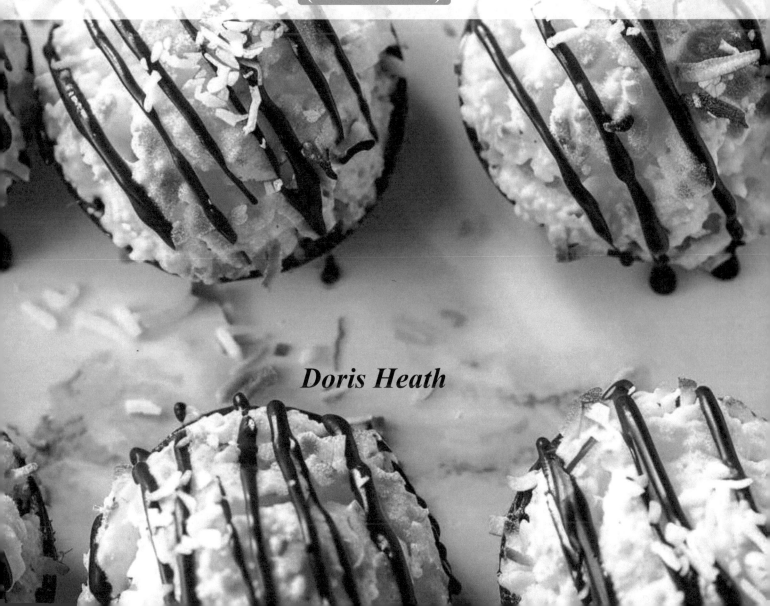

Doris Heath

Legal & Disclaimer

The content and information in this book is
consistent and truthful,
and it has been provided for informational,
educational and business purposes only.

The illustrations in the book are from the
website shutterstock.com,
depositphoto.com and freepik.
com and have been authorized.

The content and information contained
in this book has been compiled from reliable sources,
which are accurate based on the knowledge,
belief, expertise and information of the Author.
The author cannot be held liable for
any omissions and/or errors.

TABLE OF CONTENT

INTRODUCTION

Welcome to the exciting world of effortless cooking with the Ninja Flip Toaster Oven & Air Fryer! This innovative 8-in-1 appliance is designed to revolutionize your kitchen experience, offering an impressive range of functions while minimizing countertop clutter. Whether you're a home cook seeking quick, healthy meals or a foodie ready to experiment with new culinary techniques, this powerful device is your perfect kitchen companion. Its unique Flip Up & Away design not only saves space but also enhances your cooking flexibility, making it ideal for even the busiest kitchens.

At its core, the Ninja Flip Toaster Oven & Air Fryer combines convenience, versatility, and performance. Featuring functions such as air fry, air roast, bake, broil, toast, bagel, dehydrate, and pizza, this appliance empowers you to prepare a wide array of dishes with ease. Imagine achieving perfectly crispy fries with little to no oil, roasting tender vegetables in minutes, baking cookies with evenly distributed heat, or making homemade jerky with the dehydrate function. With the Ninja Flip, every meal becomes an opportunity to cook smarter, faster, and healthier.

What sets this appliance apart from traditional toaster ovens and air fryers is its thoughtfully designed accessories and precision controls. Equipped with a large air fry basket, sheet pan, wire rack, and removable crumb tray, it's engineered to simplify meal preparation while ensuring easy cleanup. The air fry basket, in particular, maximizes airflow around your food, allowing for crispy exteriors and juicy interiors without excess oil. Plus, the wire rack and sheet pan ensure even heat distribution, giving your meals a professional finish.

Another standout feature of the Ninja Flip Toaster Oven & Air Fryer is its rapid preheating and intuitive digital controls. The appliance heats up in moments, so you can start cooking almost immediately, eliminating the need for long preheating times that traditional ovens require. The control panel offers customizable temperature and time settings, enabling precise cooking. Whether you're toasting your morning bagel to golden perfection or roasting a succulent chicken, the Ninja Flip's accuracy ensures consistent results, time after time.

This cookbook is designed to help you explore the full potential of your Ninja Flip Toaster Oven & Air Fryer. Inside, you'll find recipes ranging from easy weeknight dinners to decadent desserts, all tailored to make the most of this appliance's features. Each recipe is crafted to guide you through cooking techniques such as air frying, roasting, and baking, so you can achieve delicious and healthy meals without the hassle of multiple appliances. From crispy chicken wings to perfectly roasted vegetables, you'll discover how versatile and convenient this device truly is.

Beyond just recipes, this book offers practical tips and tricks to help you adapt traditional cooking methods for the Ninja Flip. You'll learn how to adjust cooking times, temperatures, and portions to suit this powerful machine, ensuring your favorite dishes come out perfectly every time. Whether you're cooking for one or feeding a family, the Ninja Flip Toaster Oven & Air Fryer can handle it all with ease and efficiency.

So, get ready to elevate your cooking game! With the Ninja Flip Toaster Oven & Air Fryer, delicious, healthy meals are just a flip away. Whether you're air frying crispy favorites, roasting tender meats, or baking fresh pastries, this appliance makes it all possible. Let's dive in and explore the culinary possibilities that await in your kitchen!

CHAPTER 1: NAVIGATING YOUR NINJA FLIP AIR FRYER

The Ninja Flip Toaster Oven & Air Fryer is a multifunctional kitchen appliance designed to make cooking faster, easier, and healthier. Its standout feature, the Flip Up & Away capability, allows it to save valuable counter space by flipping up vertically when not in use, making it ideal for compact kitchens or those looking to maximize space. Despite its small footprint, this appliance delivers powerful, versatile performance, replacing several traditional kitchen gadgets with its 8-in-1 functionality.

With this toaster oven and air fryer, you can seamlessly switch between air frying, baking, air roasting, broiling, toasting, and even dehydrating. The large capacity air fry basket ensures your meals are cooked evenly, while the sheet pan and wire rack offer flexible cooking options for different recipes. Whether you're preparing a quick breakfast, roasting vegetables, or air frying a batch of crispy chicken wings, the Ninja Flip handles it with precision.

One of its key benefits is the ability to achieve crispy, golden results with minimal to no oil, making it a healthier alternative to deep frying. The air fry function circulates hot air evenly around food, giving it a perfect crunch without the extra calories from oil. This versatility allows home cooks to prepare a wide range of dishes, from snacks and sides to main courses and even desserts.

Additionally, the digital control panel is user-friendly, offering preset functions and customizable settings for time, temperature, and shade levels. The quick preheat feature reduces waiting time, making it a great option for busy families or anyone who needs meals prepared in a hurry. The removable crumb tray, air fry basket, and other accessories are designed for easy cleanup, making the Ninja Flip as convenient to maintain as it is to cook with.

In summary, the Ninja Flip Toaster Oven & Air Fryer is the ultimate all-in-one appliance for home cooks looking to simplify their kitchen routines without compromising on performance or quality. It offers exceptional versatility, healthy cooking options, and space-saving convenience—all in a sleek, modern design.

Advantages of the Ninja Flip Air Fryer

●Space-Saving Design

The most unique and innovative feature of the Ninja Flip Toaster Oven & Air Fryer is its Flip Up & Away capability, which allows it to be stored vertically when not in use. This is a game-changer for those with limited counter space, as it significantly reduces clutter while still providing the functionality of multiple kitchen appliances in one compact unit.

● Versatile 8-in-1 Functionality

This appliance truly shines with its 8 cooking functions, including air fry, bake, air roast, broil, toast, bagel, dehydrate, and pizza. Instead of needing separate devices for these tasks, the Ninja Flip can handle everything from making crispy air-fried chicken to dehydrating fruits or baking pizzas. This versatility makes it a one-stop solution for a wide variety of meals, saving both time and kitchen space.

● Healthier Cooking with Air Frying

One of the biggest advantages is the air fry function, which allows you to achieve crispy, fried-like textures with little to no oil. This makes the Ninja Flip ideal for those looking to cook healthier meals without sacrificing taste. You can enjoy crispy fries, wings, and other favorites without the guilt that comes with deep frying.

● Quick Preheating and Fast Cooking

The Ninja Flip Toaster Oven & Air Fryer is designed to preheat rapidly, minimizing the waiting time before you can start cooking. Its powerful convection system ensures even cooking with hot air circulating from both the top and bottom, resulting in faster cooking times compared to traditional ovens. This is perfect for busy households where quick, efficient meal preparation is a priority.

● Large Capacity in a Compact Size

Despite its compact design, the Ninja Flip offers a large cooking capacity. It can hold substantial portions—whether you're air frying a basket of veggies, roasting a whole chicken, or baking a tray of cookies—making it versatile enough to handle family meals and entertaining guests.

● Easy-to-Use Control Panel

The intuitive digital control panel allows for precise

adjustments to cooking time and temperature. With dedicated settings for each function (air fry, bake, air roast, etc.), it's easy to select the right cooking mode for your meal. The ability to customize settings ensures your food is cooked exactly the way you like it, every time.

● Simple Cleanup

Cleaning up after cooking is made simple with the removable crumb tray, non-stick air fry basket, and other dishwasher-safe accessories. This makes maintaining your Ninja Flip Toaster Oven & Air Fryer a breeze, so you can spend less time cleaning and more time enjoying your meals.

All in All, the Ninja Flip Toaster Oven & Air Fryer offers a winning combination of versatility, efficiency, and space-saving design. It's ideal for anyone looking to streamline their kitchen without compromising on the ability to prepare a wide range of delicious, healthy meals.

Versatile Functions of the Ninja Flip Air Fryer

The Ninja Flip Toaster Oven & Air Fryer is equipped with eight versatile cooking functions, allowing you to prepare a wide variety of meals with ease and precision. Each function is tailored to deliver optimal cooking results, whether you're making quick snacks, family dinners, or healthy meals. Here's an overview of each function and how it can enhance your cooking experience:

1. Air Fry

Perfect for: Making fast, extra-crispy foods with little to no added oil.
The air fry function allows you to prepare all your favorite fried foods in a healthier way. Whether it's chicken wings, French fries, or chicken nuggets, this function uses powerful, rapid hot air circulation to give your dishes that crispy exterior without the need for excess oil. It's perfect for those seeking a guilt-free alternative to deep-frying.

2. Air Roast

Perfect for: Achieving a crispy outside and tender inside.
The air roast function is ideal for cooking full-sized sheet pan meals, thicker proteins like chicken or steak, and roasted vegetables. By circulating hot air from all sides, this function ensures your food cooks evenly while retaining moisture inside, resulting in a

perfect balance of crispy exteriors and juicy interiors.

3. Bake

Perfect for: Evenly baking cookies, brownies, cakes, and more.

With the bake function, you can bake a wide variety of sweet and savory treats with precision. Whether you're whipping up a batch of cookies, baking a cake, or preparing a casserole, the even heat distribution ensures perfect results every time. It's an excellent alternative to using a full-sized oven, especially for smaller batches or quicker bake times.

4. Pizza

Perfect for: Cooking frozen or homemade pizza evenly. The pizza function is tailored to deliver perfectly cooked pizzas with crispy crusts and evenly melted toppings. Whether you're working with a frozen pizza or making one from scratch, this function ensures a balanced heat distribution, preventing soggy bases and undercooked toppings.

5. Broil

Perfect for: Broiling meat, fish, and browning the tops of casseroles.

The broil function is perfect for high-heat, top-down cooking. It's ideal for giving meats and fish a quick sear or finishing casseroles with a beautifully browned, crispy top. This function is excellent for quick-cooking dishes that need an extra touch of heat to lock in flavor or texture.

6. Toast

Perfect for: Evenly toasting up to 6 slices of bread. The toast function allows you to evenly toast multiple slices of bread to your preferred shade of doneness. Whether you like your toast light and golden or dark and crispy, the Ninja Flip's temperature control ensures that each slice is toasted to perfection, making breakfast quick and easy.

7. Bagel

Perfect for: Perfectly toasting up to 6 bagel halves. The bagel function is specially designed for toasting bagels cut-side up. It applies more heat to the cut side while gently warming the outside, giving you a perfectly crisp interior with a soft outer crust. Toast up to six halves at a time, ideal for a quick breakfast or snack.

8. Dehydrate

Perfect for: Dehydrating meats, fruits, and vegetables for healthy snacks.

The dehydrate function removes moisture from food at a low, consistent temperature, making it ideal for preserving fruits, vegetables, and meats. Use it to create healthy, homemade snacks like beef jerky, dried fruit, or vegetable chips. This function is a great way to make long-lasting, preservative-free snacks right at home.

With these eight functions, the Ninja Flip Toaster Oven & Air Fryer offers an incredible range of cooking possibilities. Whether you're looking to fry, bake, air roast, broil, or even dehydrate, this appliance has a function to match every meal you're preparing. The ability to customize each function with precise temperature and time controls ensures that your food is always cooked to perfection, no matter the dish.

Using the Control Panel

The control panel of the Ninja Flip Toaster Oven & Air Fryer is designed to be user-friendly, offering precise control over your cooking functions, temperatures, and times. Whether you're an experienced cook or a beginner, this digital interface makes it easy to navigate through the appliance's many features.

◆ Power Button

The POWER button is your starting point. Simply press it to turn the unit on or off. Once activated, the control panel lights up, allowing you to select your desired cooking function.

◆ Mode Selection (+/-) Buttons

The MODE +/- buttons let you cycle through the 8 available cooking functions, including air fry, bake, air roast, broil, toast, bagel, dehydrate, and pizza. Each mode is optimized for specific cooking needs, whether you're frying crispy foods or toasting bread to perfection. Use the +/- buttons to easily switch between these modes and select the one that suits your recipe.

◆ Temperature/Shade (+/-) Buttons

Once you've selected your mode, the TEMP/SHADE +/- buttons allow you to adjust the cooking temperature. For the toast and bagel functions, these buttons control the level of browning (shade). Whether you want your toast light or dark, or need to lower the temperature for delicate baked goods, the intuitive +/- controls offer flexibility to achieve your desired results.

◆ Time/Slices (+/-) Buttons

The TIME/SLICES +/- buttons help you set the cooking duration. For functions like toasting and bagels, these buttons also allow you to select the number of slices you're cooking, ensuring even toasting every time. For all other functions, use these buttons to adjust the cooking time based on your recipe. If you need to add more time during cooking, simply press the + button to extend the duration.

◆ Start/Stop Button

The START/STOP button is used to begin or pause your cooking process. Once you've selected the desired mode, temperature, and time, press this button to start the cooking cycle. If you need to check your food midway through, press START/STOP to pause the process without resetting the time or temperature.

◆ Preheating and Display

When using functions like air fry, air roast, or bake, the appliance will often display PRE to indicate that it is preheating. The countdown will begin once the preheating is complete. During cooking, the display will show the remaining time. If you need to flip or rotate your food, the display will prompt you, helping you achieve even cooking results.

◆ Light Button

The LIGHT button allows you to turn the oven light on or off, so you can easily check on your food without opening the door and losing heat.

◆ Flip Up Indicator

After cooking, the display will show FLIP, letting you know the appliance is ready to be flipped up for easy storage. This feature maximizes your kitchen counter space and is one of the key highlights of the Ninja Flip Toaster Oven & Air Fryer.

With its intuitive controls and easy-to-read display, the Ninja Flip Toaster Oven & Air Fryer takes the guesswork out of cooking. Whether you're adjusting temperature for a roast, selecting the perfect shade for toast, or simply starting and stopping the cooking

cycle, this control panel makes it all effortless and precise.

Using the Cooking Functions

AIR FRY

1. Press the MODE +/- buttons until "AIR FRY" lights up on the display. The default cooking time and temperature settings will appear.
2. Adjust the cooking time using the TIME/SLICES +/- buttons, up to a maximum of 1 hour. The time increases in 1-minute increments.
3. Set the temperature with the TEMP/SHADE +/- buttons, choosing between 250°F and 450°F in 5-degree increments.
4. Press the START/STOP button to begin preheating the oven.
5. Place your ingredients in the air fry basket. For items that are fatty, oily, or marinated, place the basket on the top rails while inserting the sheet pan and wire rack on the bottom rails.
6. When the unit beeps to signal it's preheated, immediately insert the basket into the upper rails. If using the sheet pan, position it on the wire rack in the bottom rails. Note: The timer starts as soon as preheating is complete. If you're not ready to cook, press the TIME + button to add more time.
7. For optimal crispiness, shake or rotate the basket halfway through the cooking cycle.
8. Once the cooking time is up, the oven will beep and display "END."

AIR ROAST

1. Press the MODE +/- buttons until "AIR ROAST" appears. The default time and temperature settings will be shown.
2. Set the cooking time using the TIME/SLICES +/- buttons, up to 2 hours. Time adjustments are made in 1-minute increments under 1 hour and 5-minute increments over 1 hour.
3. Adjust the temperature with the TEMP/SHADE +/- buttons, ranging from 250°F to 450°F in 5-degree increments. Note: Air Roasting generally cooks food faster than traditional baking. Check the Quick Start Guide for specific cook times and temperatures.
4. Press the START/STOP button to start preheating. Place your ingredients on the sheet pan. Note: Ensure ingredients are cut to similar sizes for even cooking.
5. When preheating is complete, open the oven door and place the sheet pan on the wire rack in the bottom rails. Close the door. Note: The timer starts counting down once preheating is done. If

your ingredients aren't ready, press TIME + to add more time.
6. You can open the oven door during cooking to check or flip ingredients.
7. When the cooking time finishes, the unit will beep and display "END."

BAKE
Note: Use the recommended times and temperatures for boxed foods, as they may vary with different baking accessories.
1. Press the MODE +/- buttons until "BAKE" is illuminated. The default settings will appear.
2. Adjust the time with the TIME/SLICES +/- buttons, up to 2 hours. Time changes in 1-minute increments under 1 hour and 5-minute increments over 1 hour.
3. Set the temperature using the TEMP/SHADE +/- buttons, ranging from 250°F to 450°F in 5-degree increments.
4. Press the START/STOP button to start preheating. Note: If using other baking accessories, place the wire rack in the bottom rails and put the accessory on top. Note: The timer starts after preheating. If ingredients aren't ready, press TIME + to add more time.
5. Place your ingredients on the sheet pan. When preheating is complete, place the sheet pan on the wire rack in the bottom rails and close the oven door.
6. During baking, you can open the door to check or flip your ingredients. Note: You can manually adjust the time during cooking to achieve your preferred shade.
7. When the cooking time is done, the oven will beep and show "END."

PIZZA
Note: Frozen pizzas may cook faster. Keep an eye on them and adjust the time if needed.

1. Press the MODE +/- buttons until "PIZZA" lights up. The default settings will display.
2. Set the time using the TIME/SLICES +/- buttons, up to 2 hours. Time increments are 1 minute under 1 hour and 5 minutes over 1 hour.
3. Adjust the temperature with the TEMP/SHADE +/- buttons, from 180°F to 450°F in 5-degree increments.
4. Press the START/STOP button to begin preheating.
5. Place your pizza on the sheet pan or wire rack. When the oven beeps to indicate preheating is complete, place the sheet pan on the wire rack in the bottom rails and close the door.
6. You can open the door during cooking to check on your pizza.
7. When the cooking time ends, the oven will beep and display "END."

BROIL
1. Press the MODE +/- buttons until "BROIL" is displayed. The default time and temperature settings will appear.
2. Set the time using the TIME/SLICES +/- buttons, up to 30 minutes, with 10-second increments.
3. Choose a temperature setting with the TEMP/SHADE +/- buttons: HI (450°F) or LO (400°F).
4. Place your ingredients on the sheet pan and position the pan on the wire rack in the bottom rails. Close the oven door and press the START/STOP button to start cooking. Note: No preheating is required for Broil.
5. You can open the door during broiling to check or flip your ingredients.
6. When the cooking time is up, the oven will beep and show "END."

DEHYDRATE (Not available on all models)

1. Press the MODE +/- buttons until "DEHYDRATE" lights up. The default time and temperature settings will appear.
2. Set the time with the TIME/SLICES +/- buttons, up to 12 hours, in 15-minute increments. Note: Dehydrate function does not require preheating.
3. Adjust the temperature using the TEMP/SHADE +/- buttons, from 85°F to 200°F in 5-degree increments.
4. Place ingredients in the air fry basket and position the basket on the top rails of the oven. Close the door and press the START/STOP button to start.
5. During dehydration, you can open the door to check or flip ingredients halfway through.
6. When the time is up, the unit will beep and show "END."

BAGEL

1. Press the MODE +/- buttons until "BAGEL" is illuminated. The default number of slices and shade level will display.
2. Set the number of slices using the TIME/SLICES +/- buttons; you can toast up to 6 bagel halves.
3. Adjust the shade level with the TEMP/SHADE +/- buttons. Note: No temperature adjustment for Bagel function, and the unit does not preheat. Selecting the exact number of slices is crucial to avoid over- or under-toasting. Results may vary if the unit is already warm.
4. Place bagel slices cut-side up on the wire rack in the bottom rails. Close the door and press the START/STOP button to begin cooking. No need to flip the slices during cooking.
5. When cooking is complete, the oven will beep and display "END." Note: You can adjust the time manually during cooking to achieve your preferred shade.

TOAST

1. Press the MODE +/- buttons until "TOAST" lights up. The default number of slices and shade level will display.
2. Set the number of slices with the TIME/SLICES +/- buttons; up to 6 slices can be toasted at once.
3. Choose the shade level using the TEMP/SHADE +/- buttons. Note: No temperature adjustment is available for Toast function, and the unit does not preheat. Selecting the exact number of slices is important to avoid over- or under-toasting. Results may vary if the unit is already warm.
4. Place bread slices on the wire rack in the bottom rails. Close the door and press the START/STOP button to start toasting. Flipping the slices during

cooking is unnecessary.
5. When the toast cycle finishes, the unit will beep and show "END." Note: Steam may be visible during toasting, especially with refrigerated or frozen breads.

Tips for Cleaning, Maintenance & Storage

Here is a detailed guide for the Cleaning, Maintenance & Storage of the Ninja Flip Toaster Oven & Air Fryer:

Everyday Cleaning

1. Unplug and Cool Down:
- Before cleaning, unplug the unit from the outlet and allow it to cool down completely.

2. Empty Crumb Tray and Clean Accessories:
- Slide out the crumb tray from the oven when it is in the flipped-down position.
- Clean all accessories after each use. It is recommended to hand-wash them. Note that the air fry basket and wire rack may wear more quickly if placed in the dishwasher. Avoid placing the sheet pan in the dishwasher.

3. Interior Walls:
- To clean any food splatters on the interior walls, wipe them with a soft, damp sponge. Avoid using abrasive cleaners, scrubbing brushes, or chemical cleaners as these can damage the oven.

Note: Empty the crumb tray frequently and hand-wash it when necessary.

4. Exterior and Control Panel:
- Wipe the exterior of the main unit and control panel with a damp cloth. You may use a non-abrasive liquid cleanser or mild spray solution, applying it to the sponge rather than directly to the oven surface.

Note: Do not submerge the unit in water or place it in the dishwasher.

Deep Cleaning

1. Cool Down and Unplug:
- Allow the unit to cool down, then unplug it from the outlet.

2. Remove and Wash Accessories:
- Remove all accessories, including the crumb tray.
- Wash accessories separately using a non-abrasive cleaning brush for thorough cleaning. Soak them

overnight in hot, soapy water. The air fry basket and wire rack can be placed in the dishwasher, though they may wear more quickly over time.

3. Clean Interior:
■ Wash the interior of the oven with warm, soapy water and a soft cloth. Avoid abrasive cleaners, scrubbing brushes, or chemical cleaners.

Note: Never place the main unit in the dishwasher or immerse it in water or any other liquid.

4. Hand-Wash Accessories:
■ To extend the life of the accessories, hand-wash them with warm, soapy water.

5. Dry Thoroughly:
■ Ensure all parts are thoroughly dried before returning them to the oven.

Flip-Up-and-Away Storage

1. Wait for Cooling: Do not flip the unit up while it is hot or in use. The display will show "FLIP" when the unit has cooled down and is ready to be flipped. Wait for the unit to cool before handling. Avoid unplugging the unit until "FLIP" appears; the fan will run for about 15 minutes or until the unit's temperature drops to 95°F. This is normal.

2. Lift and Flip: Use the handles on each side of the unit to lift and flip it upward.

3. Store or Deep Clean: Leave the unit in the upright position when storing or for deep cleaning. Accessories can be stored inside while the unit is in the upright position.

FAQs

1. Can I use the sheet pan instead of the air fry basket for the air fry function?

Yes, you can use the sheet pan, but be sure to flip the ingredients during cooking. The crispiness might not be as consistent as when using the air fry basket.

2. Do I need to adjust the cooking times and temperatures for traditional oven recipes?

To achieve the best results, keep an eye on your food while it cooks. Refer to the cook charts provided in the Quick Start Guide for more detailed information on cooking times and temperatures.

3. Should I add ingredients before or after preheating the oven?

It's best to add ingredients after the preheating cycle is complete, as adding them too early can affect the cooking performance.

4. Why is my food coming out undercooked or overcooked?

Make sure to wait until the preheat cycle is finished before adding food. Check the progress during cooking and remove the food when it reaches the desired level of browning. The unit cooks more quickly than a traditional oven, so monitor your food closely to prevent overcooking.

5. Can I reset the oven to its default settings?

The oven retains the last settings used for each function. To restore the default settings, press and hold the START/STOP and LIGHT buttons simultaneously for 5 seconds.

6. Why do the heating elements seem to turn on and off?

This is normal behavior. The oven adjusts the heating elements' power levels to maintain accurate temperature control for each function.

7. Why is steam coming from the oven door?

This is normal. The oven door is designed to release steam from foods with high moisture content.

8. Why is water dripping onto the counter from underneath the door?

This is a normal occurrence. Condensation from high-moisture foods (such as frozen breads) can run down the inside of the door and drip onto the counter.

9. Why is there noise coming from the control panel or back of the unit?

The fan turns on to cool the control panel when the oven is hot. This is a normal function.

10. Why does the unit seem to be running even when the power is off?

The cooling fan may continue to run after the unit has been turned off. This is normal and should stop once the unit cools to below 95°F.

11. Why does "STOP" appear on the display during cooking or when I flip the oven up during cooking?

Avoid flipping the oven up while cooking. After cooking, the display will show "FLIP" when it is cool enough to do so for storage. If "STOP" appears during cooking without flipping the unit, contact Customer Service for assistance.

CHAPTER 2: BREAKFAST

Homemade Hash Browns

🕐 **PREP TIME:** *5 MINUTES,* **COOK TIME:** *12 MINUTES,* **SERVES:** *6*

🍸 INGREDIENTS:
- 4 cups shredded potatoes (or frozen hash browns)
- 2 tbsps. canola oil
- Salt and pepper to taste
- 1 tsp. garlic powder (optional)

😋 DIRECTIONS:
1. Toss shredded potatoes with canola oil, salt, pepper, and garlic powder in a bowl.
2. Arrange the potatoes in the air fry basket in a single layer.
3. Select AIR FRY, set temperature to 400°F, and set time to 12 minutes. Press START/STOP to begin preheating.
4. When the unit has preheated, place the basket on the top rails. Close oven door.
5. After 6 minutes, toss the potatoes with tongs to ensure even cooking. Return to oven and air fry for an additional 6 minutes, until crispy.
6. Serve hot.

Smoked Salmon and Capers Bagel

🕐 **PREP TIME:** *5 MINUTES,* **COOK TIME:** *4 MINUTES,* **SERVES:** *3*

🍸 INGREDIENTS:
- 3 plain bagels, halved
- 6 ounces smoked salmon
- 3 tbsps. capers
- 3 tbsps. cream cheese
- 1 medium red onion, thinly sliced

😋 DIRECTIONS:
1. Place the bagel halves on the wire rack into the bottom rails.
2. Select BAGEL, set Time/Slices to 6 bagel halves, and set Temp/Shade to medium. Close oven door and press START/STOP to begin cooking.
3. When cooking is complete, spread cream cheese on each bagel half, then top with smoked salmon, capers, and red onion.
4. Serve immediately.

Cinnamon French Toast Sticks

🕐 **PREP TIME:** *15 MINUTES,* **COOK TIME:** *10 MINUTES,* **SERVES:** *4*

🍴 INGREDIENTS:

- Nonstick cooking spray
- 6 slices of French bread, cut into sticks
- 2 eggs
- 1 cup milk
- 1 tbsp. ground cinnamon
- 1 tbsp. sugar

🍳 DIRECTIONS:

1. Cut the French bread into sticks about 1-inch wide.
2. In a bowl, whisk together the eggs, milk, cinnamon, and sugar until well combined.
3. Dip each French bread stick into the egg mixture, ensuring all sides are coated.
4. Arrange the coated French toast sticks in the air fry basket, ensuring they are not overcrowded. Spray with nonstick cooking spray.
5. Select AIR FRY, set temperature to 350°F, and set time to 10 minutes. Press START/STOP to begin preheating.
6. When the unit has preheated, place the basket on the top rails while sliding in the sheet pan and wire rack on the bottom rails to catch any grease. Close the oven door.
7. After 5 minutes, use tongs to flip the French toast sticks. Return the basket to the oven and cook for an additional 5 minutes, until golden brown and crispy.
8. When cooking is complete, remove the French toast sticks and serve with maple syrup or powdered sugar.

Avocado and Egg Toast

🕐 **PREP TIME:** *5 MINUTES,* **COOK TIME:** *4 MINUTES,* **SERVES:** *4*

🍴 INGREDIENTS:

- 4 slices whole wheat bread
- 2 ripe avocados, mashed
- 4 hard-boiled eggs, sliced
- Salt and pepper to taste
- Red pepper flakes (optional)

🍳 DIRECTIONS:

1. Place the bread on the wire rack into the bottom rails.
2. Select TOAST, set Time/Slices to 4 slices of bread, and set Temp/Shade to medium. Close oven door and press START/STOP to begin cooking.
3. When cooking is complete, spread mashed avocado on each toast and top with sliced eggs.
4. Sprinkle salt, pepper, and red pepper flakes (if using) before serving.

Classic Buttermilk Biscuits

⏱ **PREP TIME:** *10 MINUTES,* **COOK TIME:** *12 MINUTES,* **SERVES:** *6*

🍸 INGREDIENTS:
- 2 cups all-purpose flour
- 1 tbsp. baking powder
- 1 tsp. salt
- ½ cup cold butter, cubed
- ¾ cup buttermilk

😋 DIRECTIONS:
1. In a large bowl, mix flour, baking powder, and salt. Cut in cold butter until the mixture resembles coarse crumbs. Stir in buttermilk until just combined.
2. Roll dough to ½-inch thickness and cut into 6 biscuits using a round cutter.
3. Arrange the biscuits on the greased Ninja Sheet Pan.
4. Select BAKE, set temperature to 375°F, and set time to 12 minutes. Press START/STOP to begin preheating.
5. When the unit has preheated, place the sheet pan on the wire rack on the bottom rails. Close oven door.
6. Bake until the biscuits are golden brown and fully cooked.
7. Serve warm with butter and jam.

Avocado and Hummus Bagel

⏱ **PREP TIME:** *5 MINUTES,* **COOK TIME:** *4 MINUTES,* **SERVES:** *3*

🍸 INGREDIENTS:
- 3 plain bagels, halved
- 1 cup hummus
- 2 ripe avocados, sliced
- ½ tsp. paprika
- Salt and pepper to taste

😋 DIRECTIONS:
1. Place the bagel halves on the wire rack into the bottom rails.
2. Select BAGEL, set Time/Slices to 6 bagel halves, and set Temp/Shade to medium. Close oven door and press START/STOP to begin cooking.
3. When cooking is complete, spread hummus on each bagel half, then top with avocado slices.
4. Sprinkle with paprika, salt, and pepper before serving.

Veggie and Cheese Omelet

🕐 **PREP TIME:** *5 MINUTES,* **COOK TIME:** *10 MINUTES,* **SERVES:** *4-6*

🍸 INGREDIENTS:
- 6 large eggs
- 1 cup diced red bell peppers
- ½ cup chopped spinach
- ½ cup shredded cheddar cheese
- Salt and pepper to taste

😋 DIRECTIONS:
1. In a bowl, whisk together the eggs, salt, and pepper.
2. Grease a round oven-safe dish and pour the egg mixture into it. Top with diced bell peppers, spinach, and cheddar cheese.
3. Select BAKE, set temperature to 350°F, and set time to 10 minutes. Press START/STOP to begin preheating.
4. When the unit has preheated, place the dish on the wire rack on bottom rails. Close oven door.
5. Bake until eggs are fully set and cheese is melted.
6. Slice and serve with toast or fresh fruit.

Almond Butter and Strawberry Toast

🕐 **PREP TIME:** *3 MINUTES,* **COOK TIME:** *5 MINUTES,* **SERVES:** *6*

🍸 INGREDIENTS:
- 6 slices multigrain bread
- 6 tbsps. almond butter
- 12 strawberries, sliced
- 2 tsps. honey (optional)

😋 DIRECTIONS:
1. Place the bread on the wire rack into the bottom rails.
2. Select TOAST, set Time/Slices to 6 slices of bread, and set Temp/Shade to medium. Close oven door and press START/STOP to begin cooking.
3. When cooking is complete, spread almond butter on each toast and top with strawberry slices.
4. Drizzle honey on top if desired before serving.

Breakfast Sausage Patties

🕐 **PREP TIME:** 10 MINUTES, **COOK TIME:** 10 MINUTES, **SERVES:** 4

🍷 INGREDIENTS:
- 1 lb. ground pork
- 1 tsp. salt
- ½ tsp. black pepper
- 1 tsp. sage
- 1 tsp. thyme
- 1 tsp. garlic powder
- ½ tsp. crushed red pepper flakes

🍳 DIRECTIONS:
1. In a bowl, mix ground pork with salt, pepper, sage, thyme, garlic powder, and red pepper flakes until well combined. Form into 8 small patties.
2. Arrange the patties in the air fry basket in a single layer.
3. Select AIR FRY, set temperature to 375°F, and set time to 10 minutes. Press START/STOP to begin preheating.
4. When the unit has preheated, place the basket on the top rails while sliding in the sheet pan and wire rack on the bottom rails to catch any grease during cooking. Close oven door.
5. After 5 minutes, flip the patties with tongs and continue cooking for an additional 5 minutes, until fully cooked.
6. Serve hot with eggs, toast, or biscuits.

Peanut Butter Banana Toast

🕐 **PREP TIME:** 3 MINUTES, **COOK TIME:** 3 MINUTES, **SERVES:** 2

🍷 INGREDIENTS:
- 2 slices white bread
- 2 tbsps. peanut butter
- 1 banana, sliced
- 1 tsp. honey (optional)

🍳 DIRECTIONS:
1. Place the bread on the wire rack into the bottom rails.
2. Select TOAST, set Time/Slices to 2 slices of bread, and set Temp/Shade to medium. Close oven door and press START/STOP to begin cooking.
3. When cooking is complete, spread peanut butter on each toast and top with banana slices.
4. Drizzle honey on top if desired before serving.

Spinach and Egg Cups

🕐 **PREP TIME:** *10 MINUTES,* **COOK TIME:** *12 MINUTES,* **SERVES:** *4*

🍷 INGREDIENTS:
- 6 large eggs
- 1 cup fresh spinach, chopped
- ½ cup crumbled feta cheese
- Salt and pepper to taste
- Nonstick cooking spray

😋 DIRECTIONS:
1. Grease a muffin tin or silicone molds with cooking spray.
2. In a bowl, whisk together eggs, salt, and pepper. Stir in spinach and feta.
3. Pour the mixture evenly into the muffin tin.
4. Select BAKE, set temperature to 350°F, and set time to 12 minutes. Press START/STOP to begin preheating.
5. Once preheated, place the muffin tin on the wire rack on bottom rails. Bake until the eggs are fully set.
6. Remove from the oven and let cool slightly before serving.

Bacon, Egg, and Cheese Bagel

🕐 **PREP TIME:** *10 MINUTES,* **COOK TIME:** *3 MINUTES,* **SERVES:** *2*

🍷 INGREDIENTS:
- 2 plain bagels, halved
- 4 slices cooked bacon
- 2 scrambled eggs
- 2 slices American cheese

😋 DIRECTIONS:
1. Place the bagel halves on the wire rack into the bottom rails.
2. Select BAGEL, set Time/Slices to 4 bagel halves, and set Temp/Shade to medium. Close oven door and press START/STOP to begin cooking.
3. When cooking is complete, assemble the bagels by layering scrambled eggs, bacon, and cheese.
4. Serve warm.

Sausage and Bell Pepper Breakfast Skillet

🕐 **PREP TIME:** 15 MINUTES, **COOK TIME:** 20 MINUTES, **SERVES:** 4

🍷 INGREDIENTS:
- 1 lb. breakfast sausage, sliced
- 1 red bell pepper, chopped
- 1 green bell pepper, chopped
- 1 onion, chopped
- 4 large eggs
- Salt and pepper to taste

😊 DIRECTIONS:
1. In a skillet, cook the sausage over medium heat until browned. Remove and set aside.
2. In the same skillet, cook the bell peppers and onion until softened.
3. Combine the cooked sausage and vegetables in a bowl.
4. Transfer the mixture to the Ninja Sheet Pan.
5. Crack the eggs on top.
6. Select AIR FRY, set temperature to 375°F, and set time to 20 minutes. Press START/STOP to begin preheating.
7. When the unit has preheated, place the sheet pan on the wire rack on the bottom rails. Close the oven door.
8. Cook until the eggs are set and the sausage is fully cooked.
9. When cooking is complete, remove the pan and serve hot.

Tomato Basil Toast

🕐 **PREP TIME:** 5 MINUTES, **COOK TIME:** 3 MINUTES, **SERVES:** 2

🍷 INGREDIENTS:
- 2 slices sourdough bread
- 1 medium tomato, sliced
- ¼ cup fresh basil leaves
- 2 tbsps. cream cheese
- 2 tbsps. canola oil
- Salt and pepper to taste

😊 DIRECTIONS:
1. Place the bread on the wire rack into the bottom rails.
2. Select TOAST, set Time/Slices to 2 slices of bread, and set Temp/Shade to dark. Close oven door and press START/STOP to begin cooking.
3. When cooking is complete, spread cream cheese on each toast and top with tomato slices and basil leaves.
4. Drizzle with canola oil and season with salt and pepper before serving.

CHAPTER 3: PIZZA AND SANDWICHES

BBQ Chicken Pizza

⏱ **PREP TIME:** *15 MINUTES*, **COOK TIME:** *12 MINUTES*, **SERVES:** *4*

🍸 INGREDIENTS:
- 1 (12-inch) pre-made pizza dough
- 1½ cups shredded mozzarella cheese
- 1 cup BBQ sauce
- 1 cup cooked, shredded chicken
- ½ cup red onion, thinly sliced
- 1 tbsp. canola oil

😋 DIRECTIONS:
1. Spread the BBQ sauce evenly over the pizza dough.
2. Top with shredded chicken and mozzarella cheese.
3. Scatter red onion slices over the top and drizzle with canola oil.
4. Select PIZZA, set temperature to 375°F, and set time to 12 minutes. Press START/STOP to begin preheating.
5. When unit has preheated, place the pizza on wire rack into the bottom rails. Close oven door.
6. When cooking is complete, remove from the oven and let cool for a few minutes before slicing and serving.

Caprese Sandwich

⏱ **PREP TIME:** *10 MINUTES*, **COOK TIME:** *5 MINUTES*, **SERVES:** *2*

🍸 INGREDIENTS:
- 2 ciabatta rolls
- 1 tomato, sliced
- 4 slices fresh mozzarella cheese
- ¼ cup fresh basil leaves
- 2 tbsps. balsamic glaze
- 1 tbsp. canola oil

😋 DIRECTIONS:
1. Arrange tomato slices, mozzarella cheese, and basil leaves on one half of each ciabatta roll.
2. Drizzle with balsamic glaze and canola oil.
3. Close the rolls and place them on the Ninja Sheet Pan in a single layer.
4. Select BROIL, set temperature to HI, and set time to 5 minutes. Press START/STOP to begin cooking.
5. Halfway through cooking, flip the sandwiches with tongs.
6. When cooking is complete, remove from the oven and let cool slightly before serving.

Classic Margherita Pizza

🕐 **PREP TIME:** *15 MINUTES,* **COOK TIME:** *12 MINUTES,* **SERVES:** *4*

🍴 INGREDIENTS:
- 1 (12-inch) pre-made pizza dough
- 1 cup marinara sauce
- 1½ cups shredded mozzarella cheese
- 1 cup fresh basil leaves
- 1 tbsp. canola oil
- Salt to taste

🍳 DIRECTIONS:
1. Spread the marinara sauce evenly over the pizza dough.
2. Sprinkle mozzarella cheese on top of the sauce.
3. Drizzle with canola oil and season with salt.
4. Select PIZZA, set temperature to 375°F, and set time to 12 minutes. Press START/STOP to begin preheating.
5. When unit has preheated, place the pizza on wire rack into the bottom rails. Close oven door.
6. When cooking is complete, remove the pizza from the oven and top with fresh basil leaves before serving.

Pulled Pork Sandwich

🕐 **PREP TIME:** *10 MINUTES,* **COOK TIME:** *10 MINUTES,* **SERVES:** *4*

🍴 INGREDIENTS:
- 4 hamburger buns
- 2 cups pulled pork
- ¼ cup coleslaw
- ½ cup barbecue sauce

🍳 DIRECTIONS:
1. Mix pulled pork with barbecue sauce.
2. Place the pulled pork mixture on the Ninja Sheet Pan.
3. Arrange hamburger buns next to the pork.
4. Select BROIL, set temperature to HI, and set time to 10 minutes. Press START/STOP to begin cooking.
5. Halfway through cooking, stir the pulled pork with tongs.
6. When cooking is complete, remove from the oven and let cool slightly before serving on the buns with coleslaw.

Pepperoni and Mushroom Pizza

🕐 *PREP TIME: 15 MINUTES, **COOK TIME:** 12 MINUTES, **SERVES:** 4*

🍷 INGREDIENTS:

- 1 (12-inch) pre-made pizza dough
- 1½ cups shredded mozzarella cheese
- 1 cup marinara sauce
- 1 cup sliced pepperoni
- ½ cup sliced mushrooms
- 1 tbsp. canola oil
- Salt and pepper to taste

😋 DIRECTIONS:

1. Spread the marinara sauce evenly over the pizza dough.
2. Sprinkle mozzarella cheese on top of the sauce.
3. Arrange the pepperoni slices and mushrooms on top of the cheese.
4. Drizzle with canola oil and season with salt and pepper.
5. Select PIZZA, set temperature to 375°F, and set time to 12 minutes. Press START/STOP to begin preheating.
6. When unit has preheated, place the pizza on wire rack into the bottom rails. Close oven door.
7. When cooking is complete, remove the pizza from the oven and let cool slightly before serving.

Egg Salad Sandwich

🕐 *PREP TIME: 10 MINUTES, **COOK TIME:** 5 MINUTES, **SERVES:** 2*

🍷 INGREDIENTS:

- 4 slices of bread
- 4 hard-boiled eggs, chopped
- 2 tbsps. mayonnaise
- 1 tbsp. mustard
- 1 tbsp. chopped fresh chives
- Salt and pepper to taste

😋 DIRECTIONS:

1. Mix chopped eggs with mayonnaise, mustard, chives, salt, and pepper.
2. Spread the egg salad evenly on two slices of bread.
3. Top with remaining bread slices.
4. Arrange the sandwiches on the Ninja Sheet Pan in a single layer.
5. Select BROIL, set temperature to HI, and set time to 5 minutes. Press START/STOP to begin cooking.
6. Halfway through cooking, flip the sandwiches with tongs.
7. When cooking is complete, remove from the oven and let cool slightly before serving.

Pesto and Sun-Dried Tomato Pizza

🕐 **PREP TIME:** *15 MINUTES,* **COOK TIME:** *12 MINUTES,* **SERVES:** *4*

🍸 INGREDIENTS:
- 1 (12-inch) pre-made pizza dough
- 1½ cups shredded mozzarella cheese
- ½ cup sun-dried tomatoes, chopped
- ½ cup pesto sauce
- ¼ cup sliced black olives
- 1 tbsp. canola oil

😋 DIRECTIONS:
1. Spread pesto sauce evenly over the pizza dough.
2. Sprinkle mozzarella cheese over the pesto.
3. Top with sun-dried tomatoes and black olives. Drizzle with canola oil.
4. Select PIZZA, set temperature to 375°F, and set time to 12 minutes. Press START/STOP to begin preheating.
5. When unit has preheated, place the pizza on wire rack into the bottom rails. Close oven door.
6. When cooking is complete, remove from the oven and let cool slightly before slicing and serving.

BLT Sandwich

🕐 **PREP TIME:** *10 MINUTES,* **COOK TIME:** *5 MINUTES,* **SERVES:** *4*

🍸 INGREDIENTS:
- 8 slices of bread
- 8 slices bacon
- 4 slices lettuce
- 4 slices tomato
- 4 tbsps. mayonnaise

😋 DIRECTIONS:
1. Cook the bacon on the Ninja Sheet Pan as described in the Broil section. Set aside.
2. Spread mayonnaise on each slice of bread.
3. Layer bacon, lettuce, and tomato on two slices of bread.
4. Top with the remaining bread slices.
5. Arrange the sandwiches on the Ninja Sheet Pan in a single layer.
6. Select BROIL, set temperature to HI, and set time to 5 minutes. Press START/STOP to begin cooking.
7. Halfway through cooking, flip the sandwiches with tongs.
8. When cooking is complete, remove from the oven and let cool slightly before serving.

Classic Grilled Cheese Sandwich

🕐 **PREP TIME:** *10 MINUTES,* **COOK TIME:** *5 MINUTES,* **SERVES:** *4*

🍴 **INGREDIENTS:**
- 8 slices of bread
- 4 tbsps. butter
- 4 slices cheddar cheese
- 4 slices Swiss cheese

🍳 **DIRECTIONS:**
1. Spread butter on one side of each slice of bread.
2. Place 4 slices of cheddar cheese and 4 slices of Swiss cheese between two slices of bread, buttered sides out.
3. Arrange the sandwich on the Ninja Sheet Pan in a single layer.
4. Select BROIL, set temperature to HI, and set time to 6 minutes. Press START/STOP to begin cooking.
5. Halfway through cooking, flip the sandwich with tongs.
6. When cooking is complete, remove from the oven and let cool slightly before serving.

Hawaiian Pizza with Pineapple and Ham

🕐 **PREP TIME:** *15 MINUTES,* **COOK TIME:** *12 MINUTES,* **SERVES:** *4*

🍴 **INGREDIENTS:**
- 1 (12-inch) pre-made pizza dough
- 1½ cups shredded mozzarella cheese
- ½ cup pineapple chunks
- ½ cup cooked ham, diced
- 1 cup marinara sauce
- 1 tbsp. canola oil
- Black pepper to taste

🍳 **DIRECTIONS:**
1. Spread the marinara sauce evenly over the pizza dough.
2. Sprinkle mozzarella cheese on top of the sauce.
3. Scatter ham and pineapple chunks over the cheese.
4. Drizzle with canola oil and season with black pepper.
5. Select PIZZA, set temperature to 375°F, and set time to 12 minutes. Press START/STOP to begin preheating.
6. When unit has preheated, place the pizza on wire rack into the bottom rails. Close oven door.
7. When cooking is complete, remove from the oven and let cool slightly before slicing and serving.

Four Cheese Pizza

🕐 **PREP TIME:** *15 MINUTES,* **COOK TIME:** *12 MINUTES,* **SERVES:** *4*

🍸 INGREDIENTS:
- 1 (12-inch) pre-made pizza dough
- 1 cup marinara sauce
- ½ cup shredded mozzarella cheese
- ½ cup shredded cheddar cheese
- ¼ cup grated Parmesan cheese
- ¼ cup crumbled blue cheese
- 1 tbsp. canola oil

🍳 DIRECTIONS:
1. Spread marinara sauce evenly over the pizza dough.
2. Sprinkle mozzarella, cheddar, blue cheese, and Parmesan cheeses over the sauce.
3. Drizzle with canola oil.
4. Select PIZZA, set temperature to 375°F, and set time to 12 minutes. Press START/STOP to begin preheating.
5. When unit has preheated, place the pizza on wire rack into the bottom rails. Close oven door.
6. When cooking is complete, remove from the oven and let cool slightly before slicing and serving.

Philly Cheesesteak Sandwich

🕐 **PREP TIME:** *15 MINUTES,* **COOK TIME:** *10 MINUTES,* **SERVES:** *2*

🍸 INGREDIENTS:
- 2 hoagie rolls
- 1 cup thinly sliced beef steak
- 1 cup bell peppers, sliced
- ½ cup onions, sliced
- 4 slices provolone cheese
- 1 tbsp. canola oil

🍳 DIRECTIONS:
1. Sauté bell peppers and onions in a skillet with canola oil until soft. Set aside.
2. Place thinly sliced beef steak on the Ninja Sheet Pan and arrange the hoagie rolls beside it.
3. Top the beef with bell peppers, onions, and provolone cheese.
4. Select BROIL, set temperature to HI, and set time to 10 minutes. Press START/STOP to begin cooking.
5. Halfway through cooking, flip the beef with tongs.
6. When cooking is complete, remove from the oven and let cool slightly before serving.

Green Beans with Almonds

🕐 **PREP TIME:** *10 MINUTES,* **COOK TIME:** *12 MINUTES,* **SERVES:** *4*

🍷 INGREDIENTS:
- 1 pound green beans, trimmed
- 1 tbsp. canola oil
- ¼ cup sliced almonds
- ½ tsp. garlic powder
- Salt and pepper to taste

🍳 DIRECTIONS:
1. Mix green beans with canola oil, sliced almonds, garlic powder, salt, and pepper.
2. Arrange green beans in the air fry basket, making sure they are not crowding each other.
3. Select AIR FRY, set temperature to 400°F, and set time to 12 minutes. Press START/STOP to begin preheating.
4. When unit has preheated, place the basket on the top rails. Close oven door.
5. After 6 minutes, use tongs to shake the basket. Return basket to oven and cook for an additional 6 minutes, until beans are tender and almonds are toasted.
6. When cooking is complete, serve hot.

Air Fried Brussels Sprouts

🕐 **PREP TIME:** *15 MINUTES,* **COOK TIME:** *15 MINUTES,* **SERVES:** *4*

🍷 INGREDIENTS:
- 1 lb. Brussels sprouts, halved
- 1 tbsp. canola oil
- ½ tsp. garlic powder
- ¼ tsp. red pepper flakes
- Salt to taste

🍳 DIRECTIONS:
1. Drizzle Brussels sprouts with canola oil and season with garlic powder, red pepper flakes, and salt.
2. Arrange Brussels sprouts in the air fry basket, making sure they are not crowding each other.
3. Select AIR FRY, set temperature to 400°F, and set time to 15 minutes. Press START/STOP to begin preheating.
4. When unit has preheated, place the basket on the top rails. Close oven door.
5. After 7 minutes, use tongs to shake the basket. Return basket to oven and cook for an additional 8 minutes, until crispy and browned.
6. When cooking is complete, serve hot.

Roasted Carrot and Parsnip Sticks

🕐 **PREP TIME:** 15 MINUTES, **COOK TIME:** 20 MINUTES, **SERVES:** 4-6

🍸 INGREDIENTS:
- 4 large carrots, peeled and cut into sticks
- 4 parsnips, peeled and cut into sticks
- 2 tbsps. lemon juice
- 2 tbsps. canola oil
- 1 tsp. dried thyme
- Salt and pepper to taste

🍳 DIRECTIONS:
1. Drizzle carrots and parsnips with canola oil and season with dried thyme, lemon juice, salt, and pepper.
2. Arrange vegetable mixtures in a single layer on the Ninja Sheet Pan.
3. Select AIR ROAST, set temperature to 400°F, and set time to 20 minutes. Press START/STOP to begin preheating.
4. When unit has preheated, place the sheet pan on the wire rack on bottom rails. Close oven door.
5. After 10 minutes, use tongs to stir the vegetables. Return pan to oven and roast for an additional 10 minutes, until vegetables are tender and caramelized.
6. When cooking is complete, serve hot.

Garlic Mushrooms

🕐 **PREP TIME:** 10 MINUTES, **COOK TIME:** 15 MINUTES, **SERVES:** 4

🍸 INGREDIENTS:
- 16 oz. mushrooms, sliced ¼-inch thick
- 1 tbsp. canola oil
- ½ tsp. garlic powder
- ¼ tsp. dried thyme
- Salt and pepper to taste

🍳 DIRECTIONS:
1. Drizzle mushrooms with canola oil and sprinkle with garlic powder, dried thyme, salt, and pepper.
2. Arrange mushrooms in the air fry basket, making sure they are not crowding each other.
3. Select AIR FRY, set temperature to 390°F, and set time to 15 minutes. Press START/STOP to begin preheating.
4. When unit has preheated, place the basket on the top rails. Close oven door.
5. After 7 minutes, use tongs to shake the basket. Return basket to oven and cook for an additional 8 minutes, until mushrooms are tender and slightly crispy.
6. When cooking is complete, serve hot.

Spiced Broccoli and Cauliflower

🕐 **PREP TIME:** *15 MINUTES,* **COOK TIME:** *20 MINUTES,* **SERVES:** *4*

🍷 INGREDIENTS:
- 2 cups broccoli florets
- 2 cups cauliflower florets
- 2 tbsps. canola oil
- 2 tbsps. lime juice
- 1 tsp. dried oregano
- 1 tsp. garlic powder
- 1 tsp. cumin
- ½ tsp. paprika
- Salt and pepper to taste

🍳 DIRECTIONS:
1. In a large bowl, combine broccoli and cauliflower florets with canola oil, lime juice, garlic powder, paprika, oregano, cumin, salt, and pepper.
2. Arrange broccoli and cauliflower florets in a single layer on the Ninja Sheet Pan.
3. Select AIR ROAST, set temperature to 400°F, and set time to 20 minutes. Press START/STOP to begin preheating.
4. When unit has preheated, place the sheet pan on the wire rack on bottom rails. Close oven door.
5. After 10 minutes, use tongs to stir the vegetable. Return pan to oven and roast for an additional 10 minutes, until vegetables are tender and slightly crispy.
6. When cooking is complete, serve hot.

Asparagus with Lemon Zest

🕐 **PREP TIME:** *10 MINUTES,* **COOK TIME:** *12 MINUTES,* **SERVES:** *4*

🍷 INGREDIENTS:
- 2 bunches asparagus, trimmed
- 1 tbsp. canola oil
- ½ tsp. lemon zest
- Salt and pepper to taste

🍳 DIRECTIONS:
1. In a bowl, combine asparagus with canola oil and season with lemon zest, salt, and pepper.
2. Arrange asparagus in the air fry basket, making sure they are not crowding each other.
3. Select AIR FRY, set temperature to 400°F, and set time to 12 minutes. Press START/STOP to begin preheating.
4. When unit has preheated, place the basket on the top rails. Close oven door.
5. After 6 minutes, use tongs to shake the basket. Return basket to oven and cook for an additional 6 minutes, until asparagus is tender and slightly crispy.
6. When cooking is complete, serve hot.

Simple Green Beans and Mushrooms

🕐 **PREP TIME:** *15 MINUTES,* **COOK TIME:** *18 MINUTES,* **SERVES:** *4*

🍸 INGREDIENTS:
- 2 cups green beans, trimmed
- 1 cup mushrooms, sliced
- 2 tbsps. soy sauce
- 2 tbsps. canola oil
- 1 tsp. dried basil
- ½ tsp. onion powder
- Salt and pepper to taste

😋 DIRECTIONS:
1. In a large bowl, combine green beans, mushrooms, canola oil, soy sauce, dried basil, onion powder, salt, and pepper.
2. Arrange green beans and mushrooms in a single layer on the Ninja Sheet Pan.
3. Select AIR ROAST, set temperature to 400°F, and set time to 18 minutes. Press START/STOP to begin preheating.
4. When unit has preheated, place the sheet pan on the wire rack on bottom rails. Close oven door.
5. After 9 minutes, use tongs to stir the vegetable. Return pan to oven and roast for an additional 9 minutes, until vegetables are tender and slightly crispy.
6. When cooking is complete, serve hot.

Quinoa Stuffed Bell Peppers

🕐 **PREP TIME:** *20 MINUTES,* **COOK TIME:** *20 MINUTES,* **SERVES:** *4*

🍸 INGREDIENTS:
- 4 bell peppers, cut off tops and seeded
- 1 cup cooked quinoa
- ½ cup black beans, drained and rinsed
- ½ cup corn kernels
- ¼ cup chopped tomatoes
- 1 tsp. cumin
- 1 tsp. chili powder
- ½ cup shredded cheese (optional)

😋 DIRECTIONS:
1. Mix cooked quinoa, black beans, corn, tomatoes, cumin, and chili powder in a bowl.
2. Stuff each bell pepper with the quinoa mixture, packing it down gently.
3. Arrange stuffed peppers in the air fry basket.
4. Select AIR FRY, set temperature to 400°F, and set time to 20 minutes. Press START/STOP to begin preheating.
5. When unit has preheated, place the basket on the top rails. Close oven door.
6. If using cheese, sprinkle on top of peppers during the last 5 minutes of cooking.
7. When cooking is complete, serve hot.

Herb-Crusted Cauliflower Bites with Garlic Aioli

🕐 **PREP TIME:** *10 MINUTES,* **COOK TIME:** *20 MINUTES,* **SERVES:** *4*

🍸 INGREDIENTS:

- 1 head cauliflower, cut into florets
- ½ cup breadcrumbs
- 1 tsp. dried oregano
- 1 tsp. dried thyme
- 1 tsp. garlic powder
- 1 egg, beaten

For the Garlic Aioli:
- ¼ cup mayonnaise
- 1 clove garlic, minced
- 1 tsp. lemon juice
- 1 tsp. canola oil

😋 DIRECTIONS:

1. In a bowl, mix breadcrumbs, oregano, thyme, and garlic powder.
2. Dip cauliflower florets in the beaten egg, then coat them with the breadcrumb mixture.
3. Arrange the cauliflower florets in the air fry basket without overlapping.
4. Select AIR FRY, set the temperature to 400°F, and set the time to 20 minutes. Press START/STOP to preheat.
5. Once preheated, place the basket on the top rails and close the oven door.
6. After 10 minutes, shake the basket and flip the cauliflower. Cook for another 10 minutes until crispy.
7. While the cauliflower cooks, mix mayonnaise, garlic, lemon juice, and canola oil to make the garlic aioli.
8. When cooking is complete, serve the cauliflower bites with garlic aioli.

Spicy Okra

🕐 **PREP TIME:** *10 MINUTES,* **COOK TIME:** *15 MINUTES,* **SERVES:** *4*

🍸 INGREDIENTS:

- 1 tbsp. canola oil
- 1 lb. okra, trimmed
- ½ tsp. cayenne pepper
- ½ tsp. paprika
- Salt to taste

😋 DIRECTIONS:

1. In a bowl, combine okra with canola oil, cayenne pepper, paprika, and salt.
2. Arrange seasoned okra in the air fry basket, making sure they are not crowding each other.
3. Select AIR FRY, set temperature to 400°F, and set time to 15 minutes. Press START/STOP to begin preheating.
4. When unit has preheated, place the basket on the top rails. Close oven door.
5. After 7 minutes, use tongs to shake the basket. Return basket to oven and cook for an additional 8 minutes, until crispy and tender.
6. When cooking is complete, serve hot.

Eggplant Parmesan Bites

⏱ **PREP TIME:** 20 MINUTES, **COOK TIME:** 16 MINUTES, **SERVES:** 6

🍷 INGREDIENTS:

- 2 medium eggplants, cut into bite-sized cubes
- 1 tsp. dried basil
- 1 cup breadcrumbs
- ¼ cup grated Parmesan cheese
- 1 tsp. dried oregano
- 2 eggs, beaten

🍳 DIRECTIONS:

1. Mix breadcrumbs, Parmesan cheese, dried basil, and dried oregano in a bowl.
2. Dip eggplant cubes in beaten eggs, then coat with breadcrumb mixture.
3. Arrange eggplant cubes in the air fry basket, making sure they are not crowding each other.
4. Select AIR FRY, set temperature to 400°F, and set time to 16 minutes. Press START/STOP to begin preheating.
5. When unit has preheated, place the basket on the top rails. Close oven door.
6. After 8 minutes, use tongs to shake the basket. Return basket to oven and cook for an additional 8 minutes, until golden and crispy.
7. When cooking is complete, serve hot.

Air Roasted Asparagus and Cherry Tomatoes

⏱ **PREP TIME:** 10 MINUTES, **COOK TIME:** 15 MINUTES, **SERVES:** 6

🍷 INGREDIENTS:

- 1 lb. asparagus, trimmed
- 1 cup cherry tomatoes
- 2 tbsps. canola oil
- 2 tbsps. soy sauce
- 1 tbsp. rice vinegar
- ½ tsp. garlic powder
- ½ tsp. dried rosemary
- Salt and pepper to taste

🍳 DIRECTIONS:

1. In a large bowl, combine canola oil, asparagus, cherry tomatoes, soy sauce, rice vinegar, garlic powder, dried rosemary, salt, and pepper. Mix to toss well.
2. Arrange asparagus and cherry tomatoes in a single layer on the Ninja Sheet Pan.
3. Select AIR ROAST, set temperature to 400°F, and set time to 15 minutes. Press START/STOP to begin preheating.
4. When unit has preheated, place the sheet pan on the wire rack on bottom rails. Close oven door.
5. After 7 minutes, use tongs to stir the vegetable. Return pan to oven and roast for an additional 8 minutes, until vegetables are tender and slightly caramelized.
6. When cooking is complete, serve hot.

Spicy Corn on the Cob

🕐 **PREP TIME:** *10 MINUTES,* **COOK TIME:** *30 MINUTES,* **SERVES:** *6*

🍷 INGREDIENTS:

- 6 ears corn, shucked
- 2 tbsps. canola oil
- ½ tsp. paprika
- ¼ tsp. garlic powder
- Salt to taste

🍳 DIRECTIONS:

1. In a large bowl, combine corn with canola oil and season with paprika, garlic powder, and salt.
2. Arrange corn on the cob in the air fry basket, making sure they are not crowding each other.
3. Select AIR FRY, set temperature to 400°F, and set time to 30 minutes. Press START/STOP to begin preheating.
4. When unit has preheated, place the basket on the top rails. Close oven door.
5. After 15 minutes, use tongs to turn the corn. Return basket to oven and cook for an additional 15 minutes, until corn is tender and slightly charred.
6. When cooking is complete, serve hot.

Air Roasted Sweet Potatoes and Red Onions

🕐 **PREP TIME:** *15 MINUTES,* **COOK TIME:** *24 MINUTES,* **SERVES:** *4*

🍷 INGREDIENTS:

- 2 large sweet potatoes, peeled and cut into cubes
- 1 large red onion, cut into wedges
- 2 tbsps. canola oil
- 1 tsp. smoked paprika
- ½ tsp. garlic powder
- Salt and pepper to taste

🍳 DIRECTIONS:

1. In a large bowl, mix sweet potatoes and red onions with canola oil, smoked paprika, garlic powder, salt, and pepper.
2. Arrange sweet potatoes and red onions on the Ninja Sheet Pan in the air fry basket.
3. Select AIR ROAST, set temperature to 400°F, and set time to 24 minutes. Press START/STOP to begin preheating.
4. When unit has preheated, place the sheet pan on the wire rack on bottom rails. Close oven door.
5. After 12 minutes, use tongs to stir the vegetable. Return pan to oven and roast for an additional 12 minutes, until vegetables are tender and slightly crispy.
6. When cooking is complete, serve hot.

CHAPTER 5: FISH AND SEAFOOD

Pesto Haddock

🕐 **PREP TIME:** *10 MINUTES,* **COOK TIME:** *14 MINUTES,* **SERVES:** *4*

🍸 **INGREDIENTS:**
- 4 haddock fillets (6 oz. each)
- ¼ cup pesto sauce
- 1 tbsp. canola oil
- ¼ cup grated Parmesan cheese

😋 **DIRECTIONS:**
1. Spread pesto sauce over haddock fillets and place them on the Ninja Sheet Pan. Drizzle with canola oil and sprinkle with Parmesan cheese.
2. Place the sheet pan on the wire rack on bottom rails. Close oven door.
3. Select BROIL, set temperature to LO, and set time to 14 minutes. Press START/STOP to begin cooking, until haddock is opaque and flakes easily with a fork.
4. When cooking is complete, remove the sheet pan from the oven. Serve hot.

Tender Cod with Spinach

🕐 **PREP TIME:** *10 MINUTES,* **COOK TIME:** *15 MINUTES,* **SERVES:** *4*

🍸 **INGREDIENTS:**
- 4 cod fillets (6 oz. each)
- 4 cups fresh spinach
- 2 tbsps. canola oil
- 1 tsp. dried thyme
- 1 tsp. lemon juice
- Salt and pepper to taste

😋 **DIRECTIONS:**
1. Brush cod fillets with canola oil and season with thyme, lemon juice, salt, and pepper.
2. Toss spinach with a bit of canola oil, salt, and pepper.
3. Arrange cod fillets on the Ninja Sheet Pan. Scatter spinach around the fish.
4. Select AIR ROAST, set temperature to 400°F, and set time to 15 minutes. Press START/STOP to begin preheating.
5. When unit has preheated, place the sheet pan on the wire rack on bottom rails. Close the oven door.
6. Cooking is complete when cod's internal temperature reaches 145°F and spinach is wilted. If necessary, return pan to oven and cook for additional time. When cooking is complete, remove pan from oven. Serve hot.

Lemon-Dill Halibut

🕐 **PREP TIME:** *10 MINUTES,* **COOK TIME:** *10 MINUTES,* **SERVES:** *4*

🍸 INGREDIENTS:
- 4 halibut fillets (6 oz. each)
- 2 tbsps. canola oil
- 2 tbsps. lemon juice
- 1 tbsp. dried dill
- Salt and pepper to taste

🍽 DIRECTIONS:
1. Brush halibut fillets with canola oil and lemon juice. Season with dill, salt, and pepper.
2. Arrange fillets on the Ninja Sheet Pan in a single layer. Place the sheet pan on the wire rack on bottom rails.
3. Select BROIL, set temperature to HI, and set time to 10 minutes. Press START/STOP to begin cooking.
4. Halfway through cooking, flip the fillets with tongs.
5. When cooking is complete, remove the sheet pan from the oven. Serve hot.

Roasted Salmon with Asparagus

🕐 **PREP TIME:** *10 MINUTES,* **COOK TIME:** *20 MINUTES,* **SERVES:** *4*

🍸 INGREDIENTS:
- 4 salmon fillets (6 oz. each)
- 1 bunch asparagus, trimmed
- 2 tbsps. canola oil
- 1 lemon, sliced
- 2 cloves garlic, minced
- Salt and pepper to taste

🍽 DIRECTIONS:
1. Brush salmon fillets with 1 tbsp. canola oil. Season with garlic, salt, and pepper.
2. Toss asparagus with remaining canola oil, salt, and pepper.
3. Arrange salmon fillets in the center of the Ninja Sheet Pan. Place asparagus around the salmon and add lemon slices on top of the salmon.
4. Select AIR ROAST, set temperature to 400°F, and set time to 20 minutes. Press START/STOP to begin preheating.
5. When unit has preheated, place the sheet pan on the wire rack on bottom rails. Close the oven door.
6. Cooking is complete when salmon's internal temperature reaches 145°F and asparagus is tender. If necessary, return pan to oven and cook for additional time. When cooking is complete, remove pan from oven. Serve hot.

Garlic Parmesan Shrimp

🕐 **PREP TIME:** *10 MINUTES,* **COOK TIME:** *8 MINUTES,* **SERVES:** *6*

🍸 INGREDIENTS:
- 2 lbs. large shrimp, peeled and deveined
- 3 tbsps. canola oil
- 4 cloves garlic, minced
- ½ cup grated Parmesan cheese
- 2 tsps. dried basil
- Salt and pepper to taste

🍳 DIRECTIONS:
① Toss shrimp with canola oil, garlic, Parmesan cheese, basil, salt, and pepper.
② Arrange shrimp in the air fry basket, making sure they are not crowding each other.
③ Select AIR FRY, set temperature to 390°F, and set time to 8 minutes. Press START/STOP to begin preheating.
④ When unit has preheated, place the basket on the top rails while sliding in the sheet pan and wire rack on the bottom rails to catch any grease during cooking. Close oven door.
⑤ After 4 minutes, use tongs to toss the shrimp. Return basket to oven and cook for an additional 4 minutes, until shrimp are opaque and cooked through.
⑥ When cooking is complete, remove the basket from the oven. Serve hot.

Black Cod with Miso Glaze

🕐 **PREP TIME:** *15 MINUTES,* **COOK TIME:** *10 MINUTES,* **SERVES:** *4*

🍸 INGREDIENTS:
- 4 black cod fillets (6 oz. each)
- ¼ cup miso paste
- 2 tbsps. soy sauce
- 2 tbsps. honey
- 1 tbsp. rice vinegar

🍳 DIRECTIONS:
① Mix miso paste, soy sauce, honey, and rice vinegar to make the glaze. Brush this mixture over the black cod fillets.
② Arrange fillets on the Ninja Sheet Pan in a single layer. Place the sheet pan on the wire rack on bottom rails.
③ Select BROIL, set temperature to HI, and set time to 10 minutes. Press START/STOP to begin cooking.
④ Halfway through cooking, flip the fillets with tongs.
⑤ When cooking is complete, remove the sheet pan from the oven. Serve hot.

Roasted Haddock with Cauliflower and Brussels Sprouts

🕐 **PREP TIME:** *15 MINUTES,* **COOK TIME:** *25 MINUTES,* **SERVES:** *4*

🍷 INGREDIENTS:

- 4 haddock fillets (6 oz. each)
- 1 head cauliflower, cut into florets
- 1 lb. Brussels sprouts, halved
- 2 tbsps. canola oil
- 1 tsp. paprika
- 1 tsp. dried thyme
- Salt and pepper to taste

🍽 DIRECTIONS:

1. Brush haddock fillets with canola oil and season with paprika, thyme, salt, and pepper.
2. Toss cauliflower florets and Brussels sprouts with canola oil, salt, and pepper.
3. Arrange haddock fillets on the Ninja Sheet Pan. Place cauliflower and Brussels sprouts around the fish.
4. Select AIR ROAST, set temperature to 400°F, and set time to 25 minutes. Press START/STOP to begin preheating.
5. When unit has preheated, place the sheet pan on the wire rack on bottom rails. Close oven door.
6. Cooking is complete when haddock's internal temperature reaches 145°F and vegetables are tender. If necessary, return pan to oven and cook for additional time. When cooking is complete, remove pan from oven. Serve hot.

Cajun Broiled Catfish

🕐 **PREP TIME:** *10 MINUTES,* **COOK TIME:** *12 MINUTES,* **SERVES:** *6*

🍷 INGREDIENTS:

- 6 catfish fillets (6 oz. each)
- 3 tbsps. Cajun seasoning
- 1 tbsp. canola oil
- 1 lemon, cut into wedges

🍽 DIRECTIONS:

1. Brush catfish fillets with canola oil and sprinkle with Cajun seasoning.
2. Arrange catfish fillets on the Ninja Sheet Pan in a single layer. Place the sheet pan on the wire rack on bottom rails.
3. Select BROIL, set temperature to HI, and set time to 12 minutes. Press START/STOP to begin cooking.
4. Halfway through cooking, flip the catfish fillets with tongs.
5. When cooking is complete, remove the sheet pan from the oven. Serve with lemon wedges.

Garlic Shrimp with Broccoli

⏱ **PREP TIME:** *10 MINUTES,* **COOK TIME:** *15 MINUTES,* **SERVES:** *4*

🍽 INGREDIENTS:

- 1 lb. large shrimp, peeled and deveined
- 1 large head broccoli, cut into florets
- 2 tbsps. canola oil
- 1 tsp. paprika
- 1 tsp. garlic powder
- Salt and pepper to taste

🍳 DIRECTIONS:

1. Toss shrimp with 1 tbsp. canola oil, paprika, garlic powder, salt, and pepper.
2. Toss broccoli florets with remaining canola oil, salt, and pepper.
3. Arrange shrimp in the center of the Ninja Sheet Pan. Place broccoli around the shrimp.
4. Select AIR ROAST, set temperature to 400°F, and set time to 15 minutes. Press START/STOP to begin preheating.
5. When unit has preheated, place the sheet pan on the wire rack on bottom rails. Close the oven door.
6. Cooking is complete when shrimp is pink and opaque, and broccoli is tender. If necessary, return pan to oven and cook for additional time. When cooking is complete, remove pan from oven. Serve hot.

Mahi-Mahi with Lime and Cilantro

⏱ **PREP TIME:** *10 MINUTES,* **COOK TIME:** *12 MINUTES,* **SERVES:** *6*

🍽 INGREDIENTS:

- 6 mahi-mahi fillets (6 oz. each)
- 2 tbsps. canola oil
- 2 tbsps. lime juice
- 2 tbsps. chopped fresh cilantro
- Salt and pepper to taste

🍳 DIRECTIONS:

1. Brush mahi-mahi fillets with canola oil and lime juice. Season with cilantro, salt, and pepper.
2. Arrange fillets on the Ninja Sheet Pan in a single layer. Place the sheet pan on the wire rack on bottom rails.
3. Select BROIL, set temperature to HI, and set time to 12 minutes. Press START/STOP to begin cooking.
4. Halfway through cooking, flip the fillets with tongs.
5. When cooking is complete, remove the sheet pan from the oven. Serve hot.

Broiled Tuna Steaks with Soy-Ginger Marinade

🕐 *PREP TIME: 15 MINUTES, PLUS 10 MINUTES MARINATING TIME, **COOK TIME:** 8 MINUTES, **SERVES:** 6*

🍸 **INGREDIENTS:**

- 6 tuna steaks (6 oz. each)
- ¼ cup soy sauce
- 2 tbsps. ginger, grated
- 2 tbsps. honey
- 1 tbsp. sesame oil
- 1 clove garlic, minced

🍽 **DIRECTIONS:**

1. Mix soy sauce, ginger, honey, sesame oil, and garlic. Marinate tuna steaks in the mixture for at least 10 minutes.
2. Arrange tuna steaks on the Ninja Sheet Pan in a single layer. Place the sheet pan on the wire rack on bottom rails.
3. Select BROIL, set temperature to HI, and set time to 8 minutes. Press START/STOP to begin cooking.
4. Halfway through cooking, flip the tuna steaks with tongs.
5. When cooking is complete, remove the sheet pan from the oven. Serve hot.

Scallops with Green Beans

🕐 *PREP TIME: 10 MINUTES, **COOK TIME:** 15 MINUTES, **SERVES:** 4*

🍸 **INGREDIENTS:**

- 1 lb. sea scallops
- 1 bag green beans (12 oz.), trimmed
- 2 tbsps. canola oil
- 1 tsp. dried rosemary
- 1 tsp. lemon zest
- Salt and pepper to taste

🍽 **DIRECTIONS:**

1. Brush scallops with 1 tbsp. canola oil and season with rosemary, lemon zest, salt, and pepper.
2. Toss green beans with remaining canola oil, salt, and pepper.
3. Arrange scallops in the center of the Ninja Sheet Pan. Place green beans around the scallops.
4. Select AIR ROAST, set temperature to 400°F, and set time to 15 minutes. Press START/STOP to begin preheating.
5. When unit has preheated, place the sheet pan on the wire rack on bottom rails. Close the oven door.
6. Cooking is complete when scallops are opaque and green beans are tender. If necessary, return pan to oven and cook for additional time. When cooking is complete, remove pan from oven. Serve hot.

Broiled Sea Bass with Garlic and Lemon

PREP TIME: 10 MINUTES, *COOK TIME: 10 MINUTES,* *SERVES: 4*

INGREDIENTS:
- 4 sea bass fillets (6 oz. each)
- 2 tbsps. canola oil
- 3 cloves garlic, minced
- 1 lemon, sliced
- Salt and pepper to taste

DIRECTIONS:
1. Brush sea bass fillets with canola oil and sprinkle with minced garlic, salt, and pepper. Top with lemon slices.
2. Arrange fillets on the Ninja Sheet Pan in a single layer. Place the sheet pan on the wire rack on bottom rails.
3. Select BROIL, set temperature to HI, and set time to 10 minutes. Press START/STOP to begin cooking.
4. Halfway through cooking, flip the fillets with tongs.
5. When cooking is complete, remove the sheet pan from the oven. Serve hot.

Mediterranean Herbed Swordfish

PREP TIME: 10 MINUTES, *COOK TIME: 12 MINUTES,* *SERVES: 4*

INGREDIENTS:
- 4 swordfish steaks (6 oz. each)
- 2 tbsps. canola oil
- 1 tbsp. dried oregano
- 1 tbsp. dried basil
- 1 tsp. garlic powder
- Salt and pepper to taste

DIRECTIONS:
1. Brush swordfish steaks with canola oil and season with oregano, basil, garlic powder, salt, and pepper.
2. Arrange swordfish steaks on the Ninja Sheet Pan in a single layer. Place the sheet pan on the wire rack on bottom rails.
3. Select BROIL, set temperature to HI, and set time to 12 minutes. Press START/STOP to begin cooking.
4. Halfway through cooking, flip the swordfish steaks with tongs.
5. When cooking is complete, remove the sheet pan from the oven. Serve hot.

CHAPTER 6: POULTRY

Lemon Pepper Chicken Drumsticks

🕐 **PREP TIME:** *10 MINUTES,* **COOK TIME:** *30 MINUTES,* **SERVES:** *6*

🍸 INGREDIENTS:
- 6 chicken drumsticks
- 2 tbsps. canola oil
- 1 tbsp. lemon zest
- 1 tsp. lemon juice
- 1 tsp. black pepper
- ½ tsp. salt
- ½ tsp. paprika

😋 DIRECTIONS:
1. Brush drumsticks with canola oil. Season with lemon zest, lemon juice, black pepper, salt, and paprika.
2. Arrange drumsticks on the Ninja Sheet Pan in a single layer. Place the sheet pan on the wire rack on bottom rails.
3. Select BROIL, set temperature to HI, and set time to 30 minutes. Press START/STOP to begin cooking.
4. Halfway through cooking, flip drumsticks with tongs.
5. When cooking is complete, the internal temperature should reach 165°F. Serve hot.

Crispy Buttermilk Chicken Tenders

🕐 **PREP TIME:** *15 MINUTES,* **COOK TIME:** *20 MINUTES,* **SERVES:** *4*

🍸 INGREDIENTS:
- 1 lb. chicken tenders
- 1 cup buttermilk
- 1 cup all-purpose flour
- 1 cup breadcrumbs
- 1 tsp. paprika
- ½ tsp. garlic powder
- ½ tsp. onion powder
- ½ tsp. salt
- ¼ tsp. black pepper
- Nonstick cooking spray

😋 DIRECTIONS:
1. Dip chicken tenders in buttermilk, then coat with a mixture of flour, breadcrumbs, paprika, garlic powder, onion powder, salt, and black pepper.
2. Arrange chicken tenders in the air fry basket in a single layer. Spray lightly with cooking spray.
3. Select AIR FRY, set temperature to 375°F, and set time to 20 minutes. Press START/STOP to begin preheating.
4. When unit has preheated, place basket on top rails. Close oven door.
5. After 10 minutes, use tongs to flip chicken tenders. Return basket to oven and cook for an additional 10 minutes, until golden brown and crispy.
6. When cooking is complete, serve hot.

Roasted Chicken with Potatoes and Peppers

🕐 **PREP TIME:** *15 MINUTES,* **COOK TIME:** *25 MINUTES,* **SERVES:** *6*

🍸 INGREDIENTS:
- 6 boneless, skinless chicken thighs
- 2 cups diced potatoes
- 2 cups sliced bell peppers (red, yellow, or green)
- 2 tbsps. canola oil
- 1 tsp. dried Italian seasoning
- ½ tsp. garlic powder
- ½ tsp. salt
- ¼ tsp. black pepper

🍳 DIRECTIONS:
1. Toss chicken thighs, diced potatoes, and bell peppers with canola oil, dried Italian seasoning, garlic powder, salt, and black pepper.
2. Arrange chicken thighs, potatoes, and peppers on the Ninja Sheet Pan in a single layer.
3. Select AIR ROAST, set temperature to 390°F, and set time to 25 minutes. Press START/STOP to begin preheating.
4. When unit has preheated, place the sheet pan on the wire rack on bottom rails. Close oven door.
5. After 15 minutes, use tongs to stir potatoes and peppers and flip chicken thighs. Return pan to oven and cook for an additional 10 minutes.
6. When cooking is complete, the chicken should be cooked through, and the potatoes and peppers tender. Serve hot.

Buffalo Chicken Wings

🕐 **PREP TIME:** *15 MINUTES,* **COOK TIME:** *25 MINUTES,* **SERVES:** *6*

🍸 INGREDIENTS:
- 2 lbs. chicken wings
- ¼ cup hot sauce
- 2 tbsps. melted butter
- ½ tsp. garlic powder
- ¼ tsp. salt
- ¼ tsp. black pepper

🍳 DIRECTIONS:
1. Toss chicken wings in hot sauce, melted butter, garlic powder, salt, and black pepper.
2. Arrange wings in the air fry basket in a single layer.
3. Select AIR FRY, set temperature to 400°F, and set time to 25 minutes. Press START/STOP to begin preheating.
4. When unit has preheated, place the basket on the top rails while sliding in the sheet pan and wire rack on the bottom rails to catch any grease during cooking. Close oven door.
5. After 12 minutes, use tongs to flip wings. Return basket to oven and cook for an additional 13 minutes.
6. When cooking is complete, the wings should be crispy and well-coated. Serve hot.

Parmesan Crusted Chicken Breasts

🕐 **PREP TIME:** *15 MINUTES,* **COOK TIME:** *20 MINUTES,* **SERVES:** *4*

🍽 INGREDIENTS:

- Nonstick cooking spray
- 4 boneless, skinless chicken breasts
- ½ cup grated Parmesan cheese
- ½ cup breadcrumbs
- 1 tsp. dried Italian seasoning
- ½ tsp. garlic powder
- ¼ tsp. salt
- ¼ tsp. black pepper
- 1 egg, beaten

🍳 DIRECTIONS:

1. In a shallow bowl, combine Parmesan cheese, breadcrumbs, Italian seasoning, garlic powder, salt, and black pepper.
2. Dip chicken breasts in beaten egg, then coat with Parmesan mixture.
3. Arrange chicken breasts in the air fry basket in a single layer and spray with cooking spray.
4. Select AIR FRY, set temperature to 375°F, and set time to 20 minutes. Press START/STOP to begin preheating.
5. When unit has preheated, place the basket on the top rails while sliding in the sheet pan and wire rack on the bottom rails to catch any grease during cooking. Close oven door.
6. After 10 minutes, use tongs to flip chicken breasts. Return basket to oven and air fry for an additional 10 minutes.
7. When cooking is complete, the chicken should be golden and crispy. Serve hot.

Roasted Chicken Breasts and Carrots

🕐 **PREP TIME:** *10 MINUTES,* **COOK TIME:** *22 MINUTES,* **SERVES:** *4*

🍽 INGREDIENTS:

- 4 boneless, skinless chicken breasts
- 2 cups baby carrots
- 2 tbsps. canola oil
- 1 tsp. dried rosemary
- ½ tsp. garlic powder
- ½ tsp. onion powder
- ¼ tsp. salt
- ¼ tsp. black pepper

🍳 DIRECTIONS:

1. Toss chicken breasts and baby carrots with canola oil, dried rosemary, garlic powder, onion powder, salt, and black pepper.
2. Arrange chicken breasts and carrots on the Ninja Sheet Pan in a single layer.
3. Select AIR ROAST, set temperature to 375°F, and set time to 22 minutes. Press START/STOP to begin preheating.
4. When unit has preheated, place the sheet pan on the wire rack on bottom rails. Close oven door.
5. After 11 minutes, use tongs to stir carrots and flip chicken. Return pan to oven and cook for an additional 11 minutes.
6. When cooking is complete, the chicken should be golden and cooked through, and the carrots tender. Serve hot.

Honey Garlic Chicken Drumsticks

🕐 **PREP TIME:** *15 MINUTES,* **COOK TIME:** *30 MINUTES,* **SERVES:** *6*

🍽 INGREDIENTS:

- 1 tbsp. canola oil
- 6 chicken drumsticks
- ¼ cup honey
- 2 tbsps. soy sauce
- 2 cloves garlic, minced
- ½ tsp. ground ginger
- ¼ tsp. black pepper

🍳 DIRECTIONS:

1. In a bowl, mix honey, soy sauce, minced garlic, canola oil, ground ginger, and black pepper. Toss drumsticks in the mixture.
2. Arrange drumsticks in the air fry basket in a single layer.
3. Select AIR FRY, set temperature to 390°F, and set time to 30 minutes. Press START/STOP to begin preheating.
4. When unit has preheated, place the basket on the top rails while sliding in the sheet pan and wire rack on the bottom rails to catch any grease during cooking. Close oven door.
5. After 15 minutes, use tongs to flip drumsticks. Return basket to oven and cook for an additional 15 minutes.
6. When cooking is complete, the drumsticks should be caramelized and cooked through. Serve hot.

Teriyaki Chicken Skewers

🕐 **PREP TIME:** *20 MINUTES,* **COOK TIME:** *15 MINUTES,* **SERVES:** *4*

🍽 INGREDIENTS:

- 1 lb. chicken breast, cut into bite-sized pieces
- ¼ cup teriyaki sauce
- 1 tbsp. canola oil
- 1 tsp. sesame seeds
- ½ tsp. garlic powder
- ¼ tsp. black pepper

🍳 DIRECTIONS:

1. Toss chicken pieces in teriyaki sauce and canola oil. Thread onto skewers.
2. Arrange skewers on the Ninja Sheet Pan in a single layer. Place the sheet pan on the wire rack on bottom rails.
3. Select BROIL, set temperature to HI, and set time to 15 minutes. Press START/STOP to begin cooking.
4. Halfway through cooking, turn skewers with tongs and brush with additional teriyaki sauce.
5. When cooking is complete, the chicken should be cooked through and slightly charred. Serve hot.

Air Roasted Turkey and Green Beans

🕐 **PREP TIME:** *15 MINUTES,* **COOK TIME:** *30 MINUTES,* **SERVES:** *4*

🍸 INGREDIENTS:
- 4 turkey legs
- 2 cups trimmed green beans
- 2 tbsps. canola oil
- 1 tsp. dried sage
- ½ tsp. garlic powder
- ¼ tsp. salt
- ¼ tsp. black pepper

☕ DIRECTIONS:
1. Toss turkey legs and green beans with canola oil, dried sage, garlic powder, salt, and black pepper.
2. Arrange turkey legs and green beans on the Ninja Sheet Pan in a single layer.
3. Select AIR ROAST, set temperature to 390°F, and set time to 30 minutes. Press START/STOP to begin preheating.
4. When unit has preheated, place the sheet pan on the wire rack on bottom rails. Close oven door.
5. After 15 minutes, use tongs to stir green beans and flip turkey legs. Return pan to oven and cook for an additional 15 minutes.
6. When cooking is complete, the turkey should be golden and cooked through, and the green beans tender. Serve hot.

BBQ Chicken Breasts

🕐 **PREP TIME:** *15 MINUTES,* **COOK TIME:** *20 MINUTES,* **SERVES:** *4*

🍸 INGREDIENTS:
- 4 boneless, skinless chicken breasts
- ½ cup BBQ sauce
- 1 tbsp. canola oil
- ½ tsp. garlic powder
- ¼ tsp. salt
- ¼ tsp. black pepper

☕ DIRECTIONS:
1. Brush chicken breasts with canola oil. Season with garlic powder, salt, and black pepper.
2. Brush BBQ sauce over the chicken breasts.
3. Arrange chicken breasts in the air fry basket in a single layer.
4. Select AIR FRY, set temperature to 375°F, and set time to 20 minutes. Press START/STOP to begin preheating.
5. When unit has preheated, place the basket on the top rails while sliding in the sheet pan and wire rack on the bottom rails to catch any grease during cooking. Close oven door.
6. After 10 minutes, use tongs to flip chicken breasts. Brush with additional BBQ sauce and cook for an additional 10 minutes.
7. When cooking is complete, the chicken should be well-coated and cooked through. Serve hot.

Honey Mustard Glazed Chicken Thighs

🕐 *PREP TIME: 15 MINUTES, **COOK TIME:** 25 MINUTES, **SERVES:** 4*

🍸 INGREDIENTS:
- 1 tbsp. canola oil
- 4 bone-in, skin-on chicken thighs
- 2 tbsps. honey
- 2 tbsps. Dijon mustard
- ½ tsp. garlic powder
- ½ tsp. onion powder
- ¼ tsp. salt
- ¼ tsp. black pepper

🍳 DIRECTIONS:
1. In a small bowl, mix honey, Dijon mustard, and canola oil. Brush the mixture over the chicken thighs.
2. Season the chicken with garlic powder, onion powder, salt, and black pepper.
3. Arrange chicken thighs on the Ninja Sheet Pan in a single layer. Place the sheet pan on the wire rack on bottom rails.
4. Select BROIL, set temperature to HI, and set time to 25 minutes. Press START/STOP to begin cooking.
5. Halfway through cooking, flip chicken thighs with tongs.
6. When cooking is complete, the chicken should be caramelized and cooked through. Serve hot.

Chicken with Zucchini and Tomatoes

🕐 *PREP TIME: 10 MINUTES, **COOK TIME:** 25 MINUTES, **SERVES:** 4*

🍸 INGREDIENTS:
- 4 boneless, skinless chicken drumsticks
- 2 cups sliced zucchini
- 2 cups cherry tomatoes
- 2 tbsps. canola oil
- 1 tsp. dried basil
- ½ tsp. garlic powder
- ¼ tsp. salt
- ¼ tsp. black pepper

🍳 DIRECTIONS:
1. Toss chicken drumsticks, sliced zucchini, and cherry tomatoes with canola oil, dried basil, garlic powder, salt, and black pepper.
2. Arrange chicken drumsticks, zucchini, and tomatoes on the Ninja Sheet Pan in a single layer.
3. Select AIR ROAST, set temperature to 400°F, and set time to 25 minutes. Press START/STOP to begin preheating.
4. When unit has preheated, place the sheet pan on the wire rack on bottom rails. Close oven door.
5. After 10 minutes, use tongs to stir zucchini and tomatoes and flip chicken drumsticks. Return pan to oven and cook for an additional 15 minutes.
6. When cooking is complete, the chicken should be cooked through, and the zucchini and tomatoes tender. Serve hot.

BBQ Chicken Wings

🕐 **PREP TIME:** *15 MINUTES,* **COOK TIME:** *25 MINUTES,* **SERVES:** *4-6*

🍸 INGREDIENTS:

- 2 lbs. chicken wings
- ½ cup BBQ sauce
- 1 tbsp. canola oil
- ½ tsp. garlic powder
- ½ tsp. onion powder
- ¼ tsp. salt
- ¼ tsp. black pepper

😋 DIRECTIONS:

1. Brush wings with canola oil and toss in garlic powder, onion powder, salt, and black pepper.
2. Arrange wings on the Ninja Sheet Pan in a single layer. Brush BBQ sauce over the wings.
3. Place the sheet pan on the wire rack on bottom rails.
4. Select BROIL, set temperature to HI, and set time to 25 minutes. Press START/STOP to begin cooking.
5. Halfway through cooking, flip wings with tongs and brush with additional BBQ sauce.
6. When cooking is complete, the wings should be crispy and caramelized. Serve hot.

Spicy Paprika Chicken Thighs

🕐 **PREP TIME:** *10 MINUTES,* **COOK TIME:** *20 MINUTES,* **SERVES:** *4*

🍸 INGREDIENTS:

- 2 tbsps. canola oil
- 4 bone-in, skin-on chicken thighs
- 1 tbsp. smoked paprika
- ½ tsp. cayenne pepper
- ½ tsp. onion powder
- ½ tsp. garlic powder
- ¼ tsp. salt

😋 DIRECTIONS:

1. Brush chicken thighs with canola oil. Season with smoked paprika, cayenne pepper, garlic powder, onion powder, and salt.
2. Arrange chicken thighs on the Ninja Sheet Pan in a single layer. Place the sheet pan on the wire rack on bottom rails.
3. Select BROIL, set temperature to HI, and set time to 20 minutes. Press START/STOP to begin cooking.
4. Halfway through cooking, flip chicken thighs with tongs.
5. When cooking is complete, the chicken should be crispy and well-seasoned. Serve hot.

Lamb Ribs with Roasted Cauliflower

🕐 **PREP TIME:** *20 MINUTES,* **COOK TIME:** *35 MINUTES,* **SERVES:** *6*

🍽 INGREDIENTS:
- 2 racks of lamb ribs
- 2 tbsps. canola oil
- 3 cups cauliflower florets
- 1 tbsp. fresh rosemary, chopped
- 1 tsp. garlic powder
- Salt and pepper to taste

😋 DIRECTIONS:
1. Rub lamb ribs and cauliflower florets with canola oil, rosemary, garlic powder, salt, and pepper.
2. Place lamb ribs on the Ninja Sheet Pan in a single layer with cauliflower.
3. Select AIR ROAST, set temperature to 400°F, and set time to 35 minutes. Press START/STOP to begin preheating.
4. When unit has preheated, place sheet pan on the wire rack on bottom rails. Close oven door.
5. Cooking is complete when lamb's internal temperature reaches 160°F. If necessary, return pan to oven and cook for additional time.
6. When cooking is complete, remove pan from oven and let lamb rest for 5 minutes before slicing. Serve lamb ribs with cauliflower.

BBQ Pork Ribs

🕐 **PREP TIME:** *20 MINUTES,* **COOK TIME:** *30 MINUTES,* **SERVES:** *6*

🍽 INGREDIENTS:
- 2 racks of pork ribs
- 1 cup BBQ sauce
- 1 tbsp. paprika
- 1 tsp. garlic powder
- 1 tsp. onion powder
- Salt and pepper to taste

😋 DIRECTIONS:
1. Remove membrane from ribs and rub with paprika, garlic powder, onion powder, salt, and pepper.
2. Brush ribs with BBQ sauce.
3. Arrange ribs in the air fry basket. You may need to cut racks into smaller sections to fit.
4. Select AIR FRY, set temperature to 375°F, and set time to 30 minutes. Press START/STOP to begin preheating.
5. When unit has preheated, place the basket on the top rails while sliding in the sheet pan and wire rack on the bottom rails to catch any grease during cooking. Close oven door.
6. After 15 minutes, brush ribs with more BBQ sauce and flip with tongs. Return basket to oven and cook for an additional 15 minutes.
7. When cooking is complete, serve ribs hot with additional BBQ sauce if desired.

Beef Sirloin with Roasted Eggplant

🕐 **PREP TIME:** *15 MINUTES,* **COOK TIME:** *25 MINUTES,* **SERVES:** *6*

🍽 INGREDIENTS:
- 1½ lbs. beef sirloin
- 2 tbsps. canola oil
- 1 tbsp. fresh thyme, chopped
- 1 tsp. onion powder
- Salt and pepper to taste
- 3 cups eggplants, cubed

😋 DIRECTIONS:
1. Toss beef sirloin and eggplant cubes with canola oil, thyme, onion powder, salt, and pepper.
2. Place beef sirloin on the Ninja Sheet Pan in a single layer with eggplant cubes.
3. Select AIR ROAST, set temperature to 400°F, and set time to 25 minutes. Press START/STOP to begin preheating.
4. When unit has preheated, place sheet pan on the wire rack on bottom rails. Close oven door.
5. Cooking is complete when beef's internal temperature reaches 145°F for medium. If necessary, return pan to oven and cook for additional time.
6. When cooking is complete, remove pan from oven and let beef rest for 10 minutes before slicing. Serve beef with eggplant cubes.

Simple Lamb Kofta

🕐 **PREP TIME:** *15 MINUTES,* **COOK TIME:** *18 MINUTES,* **SERVES:** *4*

🍽 INGREDIENTS:
- 1 lb. ground lamb
- ¼ cup chopped parsley
- ¼ cup chopped onion
- 1 tsp. ground cumin
- 1 tsp. ground coriander
- ½ tsp. garlic powder
- Salt and pepper to taste

😋 DIRECTIONS:
1. In a bowl, mix ground lamb, parsley, onion, cumin, coriander, garlic powder, salt, and pepper.
2. Form mixture into 12 kofta patties.
3. Arrange kofta patties in the air fry basket in a single layer.
4. Select AIR FRY, set temperature to 375°F, and set time to 18 minutes. Press START/STOP to begin preheating.
5. When unit has preheated, place the basket on the top rails while sliding in the sheet pan and wire rack on the bottom rails to catch any grease during cooking. Close oven door.
6. After 10 minutes, use tongs to flip the kofta patties. Return basket to oven and cook for an additional 8 minutes.
7. When cooking is complete, serve kofta hot.

Roasted Beef Ribeye Steaks

🕐 **PREP TIME:** 10 MINUTES, **COOK TIME:** 20 MINUTES, **SERVES:** 4

🍸 INGREDIENTS:

- 2 tbsps. canola oil
- 4 ribeye steaks (8 oz. each)
- 1 tsp. garlic powder
- 1 tsp. onion powder
- 1 tsp. dried rosemary
- Salt and pepper to taste

😋 DIRECTIONS:

1. Rub steaks with canola oil, garlic powder, onion powder, rosemary, salt, and pepper.
2. Arrange steaks on the Ninja Sheet Pan in a single layer.
3. Select AIR ROAST, set temperature to 400°F, and set time to 20 minutes. Press START/STOP to begin preheating.
4. When unit has preheated, place sheet pan on the wire rack on bottom rails. Close oven door.
5. Cooking is complete when beef's internal temperature reaches 145°F. If necessary, return pan to oven and cook for additional time.
6. When cooking is complete, remove pan from oven. Let steaks rest for 5 minutes before serving.

Roasted Pork Ribs with Potatoes and Brussels Sprouts

🕐 **PREP TIME:** 20 MINUTES, **COOK TIME:** 40 MINUTES, **SERVES:** 6

🍸 INGREDIENTS:

- 2 lbs. pork ribs
- 2 tbsps. canola oil
- 1 tbsp. smoked paprika
- 1 tsp. onion powder
- Salt and pepper to taste
- 3 cups potatoes, cubed
- 2 cups Brussels sprouts, halved

😋 DIRECTIONS:

1. Toss pork ribs, potatoes and Brussels sprouts with canola oil, smoked paprika, onion powder, salt, and pepper.
2. Place pork ribs on the Ninja Sheet Pan in a single layer with potatoes and Brussels sprouts.
3. Select AIR ROAST, set temperature to 400°F, and set time to 40 minutes. Press START/STOP to begin preheating.
4. When unit has preheated, place sheet pan on the wire rack on bottom rails. Close oven door.
5. Cooking is complete when pork's internal temperature reaches 160°F. If necessary, return pan to oven and cook for additional time.
6. When cooking is complete, remove pan from oven and let pork rest for 5 minutes before serving. Serve pork ribs with potatoes and Brussels sprouts.

Crunchy Breaded Pork Chops

🕐 **PREP TIME:** *10 MINUTES,* **COOK TIME:** *15 MINUTES,* **SERVES:** *4*

🍸 INGREDIENTS:

- Nonstick cooking spray
- 4 pork chops, 1-inch thick
- 2 tbsps. canola oil
- ½ cup breadcrumbs
- ¼ cup grated Parmesan cheese
- 1 tsp. paprika
- ½ tsp. garlic powder
- Salt and pepper to taste

🍲 DIRECTIONS:

1. Brush pork chops with canola oil. Mix breadcrumbs, Parmesan cheese, paprika, garlic powder, salt, and pepper in a bowl. Coat pork chops with the mixture.
2. Arrange pork chops in the air fry basket in a single layer and spray with cooking spray.
3. Select AIR FRY, set temperature to 375°F, and set time to 15 minutes. Press START/STOP to begin preheating.
4. When unit has preheated, place the basket on the top rails while sliding in the sheet pan and wire rack on the bottom rails to catch any grease during cooking. Close oven door.
5. After 8 minutes, use tongs to flip the pork chops. Return basket to oven and cook for an additional 7 minutes.
6. Cooking is complete when pork's internal temperature reaches 145°F.
7. When cooking is complete, remove the basket from oven. Serve hot.

Herb Roasted Lamb Shanks

🕐 **PREP TIME:** *20 MINUTES,* **COOK TIME:** *45 MINUTES,* **SERVES:** *4*

🍸 INGREDIENTS:

- 4 lamb shanks
- 2 tbsps. canola oil
- 1 tbsp. fresh thyme, chopped
- 1 tbsp. fresh rosemary, chopped
- 1 tsp. garlic powder
- 1 tsp. onion powder
- Salt and pepper to taste

🍲 DIRECTIONS:

1. Rub lamb shanks with canola oil, thyme, rosemary, garlic powder, onion powder, salt, and pepper.
2. Arrange lamb shanks on the Ninja Sheet Pan in a single layer.
3. Select AIR ROAST, set temperature to 400°F, and set time to 45 minutes. Press START/STOP to begin preheating.
4. When unit has preheated, place sheet pan on the wire rack on bottom rails. Close oven door.
5. Cooking is complete when lamb's internal temperature reaches 160°F. If necessary, return pan to oven and cook for additional time.
6. When cooking is complete, remove pan from oven and let rest for 10 minutes before serving.

Pork Chops with Pumpkins

PREP TIME: *15 MINUTES,* **COOK TIME:** *25 MINUTES,* **SERVES:** *6*

INGREDIENTS:

- 6 pork chops
- 2 tbsps. canola oil
- 3 cups pumpkin, diced
- 1 tbsp. dried oregano
- 1 tsp. garlic powder
- Salt and pepper to taste

DIRECTIONS:

1. Rub pork chops, diced pumpkins with canola oil, oregano, garlic powder, salt, and pepper.
2. Arrange diced pumpkins on the Ninja Sheet Pan in a single layer.
3. Place pork chops on the Ninja Sheet Pan in a single layer with pumpkins.
4. Select AIR ROAST, set temperature to 400°F, and set time to 25 minutes. Press START/STOP to begin preheating.
5. When unit has preheated, place sheet pan on the wire rack on bottom rails. Close oven door.
6. Cooking is complete when pork's internal temperature reaches 145°F. If necessary, return pan to oven and cook for additional time.
7. When cooking is complete, remove pan from oven and let pork rest for 5 minutes before serving. Serve pork chops with pumpkins.

Air Fried Beef Meatballs

PREP TIME: *20 MINUTES,* **COOK TIME:** *15 MINUTES,* **SERVES:** *4*

INGREDIENTS:

- 1 lb. ground beef
- 1 egg
- ¼ cup breadcrumbs
- ¼ cup grated Parmesan cheese
- 1 tbsp. chopped parsley
- ½ tsp. garlic powder
- ½ tsp. onion powder
- Salt and pepper to taste

DIRECTIONS:

1. In a bowl, mix ground beef, breadcrumbs, Parmesan cheese, egg, parsley, garlic powder, onion powder, salt, and pepper.
2. Form mixture into 12 meatballs.
3. Arrange meatballs in the air fry basket in a single layer.
4. Select AIR FRY, set temperature to 375°F, and set time to 15 minutes. Press START/STOP to begin preheating.
5. When unit has preheated, place the basket on the top rails while sliding in the sheet pan and wire rack on the bottom rails to catch any grease during cooking. Close oven door.
6. After 7 minutes, use tongs to flip the meatballs. Return basket to oven and cook for an additional 8 minutes.
7. When cooking is complete, serve meatballs hot.

Herbed Roasted Pork Tenderloin

⏱ **PREP TIME:** *15 MINUTES,* **COOK TIME:** *25 MINUTES,* **SERVES:** *4*

🍽 INGREDIENTS:
- 1 lb. pork tenderloin
- 2 tbsps. canola oil
- 1 tsp. dried thyme
- ½ tsp. garlic powder
- ½ tsp. onion powder
- Salt and pepper to taste

🍳 DIRECTIONS:
1. Rub pork tenderloin with canola oil, thyme, garlic powder, onion powder, salt, and pepper.
2. Arrange pork tenderloin on the Ninja Sheet Pan in a single layer.
3. Select BROIL, set temperature to LO, and set time to 25 minutes. Press START/STOP to begin preheating.
4. When unit has preheated, place sheet pan on the wire rack on bottom rails. Close oven door.
5. Cooking is complete when pork's internal temperature reaches 145°F. If necessary, return pan to oven and cook for additional time.
6. When cooking is complete, remove pan from oven. Let tenderloin rest for 5 minutes before slicing.

Air Fried Lamb Chops

⏱ **PREP TIME:** *10 MINUTES,* **COOK TIME:** *15 MINUTES,* **SERVES:** *4*

🍽 INGREDIENTS:
- 8 lamb chops
- 2 tbsps. canola oil
- 1 tbsp. fresh rosemary, chopped
- 1 tsp. garlic powder
- Salt and pepper to taste

🍳 DIRECTIONS:
1. Rub lamb chops with canola oil, rosemary, garlic powder, salt, and pepper.
2. Arrange lamb chops in the air fry basket in a single layer.
3. Select AIR FRY, set temperature to 375°F, and set time to 15 minutes. Press START/STOP to begin preheating.
4. When unit has preheated, place the basket on the top rails while sliding in the sheet pan and wire rack on the bottom rails to catch any grease during cooking. Close oven door.
5. After 8 minutes, use tongs to flip the lamb chops. Return basket to oven and cook for an additional 7 minutes.
6. When cooking is complete, serve lamb chops hot.

Tasty Beef Tacos

🕐 **PREP TIME:** *15 MINUTES,* **COOK TIME:** *15 MINUTES,* **SERVES:** *4*

🍽 INGREDIENTS:

- 1 lb. ground beef
- 1 packet taco seasoning
- 8 small taco shells
- 1 cup shredded lettuce
- 1 cup diced tomatoes
- 1 cup shredded cheddar cheese

🍳 DIRECTIONS:

① Cook ground beef in a skillet over medium heat until browned. Drain fat and mix in taco seasoning.
② Arrange taco shells in the air fry basket. Fill each taco shell with seasoned beef.
③ Select AIR FRY, set temperature to 375°F, and set time to 10 minutes. Press START/STOP to begin preheating.
④ When unit has preheated, place the basket on the top rails while sliding in the sheet pan and wire rack on the bottom rails to catch any grease during cooking. Close oven door.
⑤ After 5 minutes, remove basket and top tacos with lettuce, tomatoes, and cheese. Return basket to oven and cook for an additional 5 minutes.
⑥ When cooking is complete, serve tacos hot.

Lamb Leg with Roasted Sweet Potatoes and Mushrooms

🕐 **PREP TIME:** *20 MINUTES,* **COOK TIME:** *40 MINUTES,* **SERVES:** *6*

🍽 INGREDIENTS:

- 2 lbs. lamb leg
- 2 tbsps. canola oil
- 1 tbsp. fresh thyme, chopped
- 1 tsp. onion powder
- Salt and pepper to taste
- 3 cups sweet potatoes, cubed
- 2 cups mushrooms, sliced

🍳 DIRECTIONS:

① Toss lamb leg, cubed sweet potatoes and sliced mushrooms, with canola oil, thyme, onion powder, salt, and pepper.
② Place lamb leg on the Ninja Sheet Pan in a single layer with sweet potatoes and mushrooms.
③ Select AIR ROAST, set temperature to 400°F, and set time to 40 minutes. Press START/STOP to begin preheating.
④ When unit has preheated, place sheet pan on the wire rack on bottom rails. Close oven door.
⑤ Cooking is complete when lamb's internal temperature reaches 160°F. If necessary, return pan to oven and cook for additional time.
⑥ When cooking is complete, remove pan from oven and let lamb rest for 10 minutes before slicing. Serve lamb leg with sweet potatoes and mushrooms.

CHAPTER 8: SNACKS AND DEHYDRATED FOODS

Herb-infused Kale Chips

🕐 **PREP TIME:** *10 MINUTES,* **COOK TIME:** *4 HOURS,* **SERVES:** *4*

🍸 INGREDIENTS:
- 1 bunch kale, stems removed, torn into pieces
- 2 tbsps. canola oil
- 1 tsp. garlic powder
- 1 tsp. onion powder
- ½ tsp. sea salt

😋 DIRECTIONS:
1. Toss the kale pieces in canola oil, garlic powder, onion powder, and sea salt until evenly coated.
2. Arrange kale in the air fry basket in a single layer, ensuring no overlap. Place the basket on the top rails.
3. Select DEHYDRATE, set the temperature to 135°F, and set the time to 4 hours. Close the oven door and press START/STOP to begin cooking.
4. Flip the kale halfway through for even drying.
5. Once crispy, remove the kale chips and allow them to cool before serving or storing.

Tasty Sweet Potato Wedges with Smoky BBQ Dip

🕐 **PREP TIME:** *10 MINUTES,* **COOK TIME:** *25 MINUTES,* **SERVES:** *4*

🍸 INGREDIENTS:
- Nonstick cooking spray.
- 1 tbsp. canola oil
- 2 large sweet potatoes, cut into wedges
- 1 tsp. smoked paprika
- ½ tsp. garlic powder
- ½ tsp. salt

For the Smoky BBQ Dip:
- ¼ cup BBQ sauce
- 1 tsp. smoked paprika
- 1 tsp. honey
- 1 tsp. apple cider vinegar

😋 DIRECTIONS:
1. Toss sweet potato wedges with canola oil, smoked paprika, garlic powder, and salt in a bowl.
2. Arrange the sweet potato wedges in the air fry basket in a single layer and spray with nonstick cooking spray.
3. Select AIR FRY, set the temperature to 375°F, and set the time to 25 minutes. Press START/STOP to preheat.
4. Once preheated, insert the basket on the top rails.
5. After 12 minutes, shake the basket to flip the wedges. Air fry for another 13 minutes until crispy.
6. While the wedges cook, mix BBQ sauce, smoked paprika, honey, and apple cider vinegar to make the smoky BBQ dip.
7. When cooking is complete, serve the sweet potato wedges with smoky BBQ dip.

Garlic Parmesan Breadsticks

🕐 **PREP TIME:** *10 MINUTES,* **COOK TIME:** *12 MINUTES,* **SERVES:** *4*

🍴 INGREDIENTS:
- Nonstick cooking spray
- 1 package refrigerated breadstick dough
- 1 tbsp. melted butter
- 2 tbsps. grated Parmesan cheese
- 1 tsp. garlic powder

🍳 DIRECTIONS:
1. Cut the breadstick dough into 8 sticks.
2. Brush each breadstick with melted butter and sprinkle with Parmesan cheese and garlic powder.
3. Arrange the breadsticks in the air fry basket in a single layer and spray with nonstick cooking spray.
4. Select AIR FRY, set temperature to 375°F, and set time to 12 minutes. Press START/STOP to begin preheating.
5. When unit has preheated, place the basket on the top rails. Close oven door.
6. After 6 minutes, use tongs to flip the breadsticks. Return basket to oven and cook for an additional 6 minutes, until golden and crispy.
7. When cooking is complete, remove from the air fryer and serve warm.

Classic Beef Jerky Strips

🕐 **PREP TIME:** *20 MINUTES, PLUS 4 HOURS MARINATING TIME,* **COOK TIME:** *6 HOURS,* **SERVES:** *6*

🍴 INGREDIENTS:
- 1½ lbs. beef round or flank steak, sliced into thin strips
- ¼ cup soy sauce
- 1 tbsp. Worcestershire sauce
- 1 tsp. garlic powder
- 1 tsp. onion powder
- 1 tsp. smoked paprika
- ½ tsp. black pepper

🍳 DIRECTIONS:
1. Mix soy sauce, Worcestershire sauce, garlic powder, onion powder, smoked paprika, and black pepper in a bowl.
2. Add beef strips to the marinade and refrigerate for 4 hours.
3. Arrange beef strips in the air fry basket, making sure they are not crowding each other. Place the basket on the top rails while sliding in the sheet pan and wire rack on the bottom rails.
4. Select DEHYDRATE, set temperature to 150°F, and set time to 6 hours. Close the oven door and press START/STOP to begin cooking.
5. Halfway through cooking, flip the beef strips with tongs.
6. When cooking is complete, remove the jerky and allow it to cool before storing.

Golden Tater Tots

🕐 **PREP TIME:** *5 MINUTES,* **COOK TIME:** *22 MINUTES,* **SERVES:** *4*

🍸 INGREDIENTS:
- 1 bag (32 oz.) frozen tater tots
- Ketchup for serving

😋 DIRECTIONS:
1. Arrange the tater tots in the air fry basket in a single layer without overcrowding.
2. Select AIR FRY, set the temperature to 360°F, and set the time to 22 minutes. Press START/STOP to preheat.
3. Once preheated, insert the basket on the top rails and close the oven door.
4. After 11 minutes, shake the basket to flip the tots, then cook for an additional 11 minutes until crispy and golden.
5. Serve the golden tater tots with ketchup on the side.

Sweet Mango Slices

🕐 **PREP TIME:** *10 MINUTES,* **COOK TIME:** *8 HOURS,* **SERVES:** *6*

🍸 INGREDIENTS:
- 3 large ripe mangoes, peeled and sliced into ¼-inch strips

😋 DIRECTIONS:
1. Pat the mango slices dry with a paper towel to remove excess moisture.
2. Arrange the mango slices in the air fry basket without overlapping. Place the basket on the top rails.
3. Select DEHYDRATE, set the temperature to 135°F, and set the time to 8 hours. Close the oven door and press START/STOP to begin cooking.
4. Flip the mango slices halfway through the drying process.
5. Once dried, let the mango slices cool before serving or storing.

Fish Sticks with Lemon Dill Aioli

🕐 *PREP TIME: 5 MINUTES, COOK TIME: 16 MINUTES, SERVES: 4*

🍸 **INGREDIENTS:**

- 1 bag (24.5 oz.) frozen fish sticks

For the Lemon Dill Aioli:

- ¼ cup mayonnaise
- 1 tsp. lemon zest
- 1 tsp. lemon juice
- ½ tsp. dried dill
- 1 clove garlic, minced

😋 **DIRECTIONS:**

1. Arrange the frozen fish sticks in the air fry basket in a single layer.
2. Select AIR FRY, set the temperature to 400°F, and set the time to 16 minutes. Press START/STOP to preheat.
3. Once preheated, place the basket on the top rails and the sheet pan below.
4. After 8 minutes, use tongs to flip the fish sticks. Return to the oven for another 8 minutes until crispy.
5. Meanwhile, mix mayonnaise, lemon zest, lemon juice, dill, and minced garlic in a small bowl to make the lemon dill aioli.
6. When cooking is complete, serve the fish sticks with the lemon dill aioli for dipping.

Healthy Kiwi Chips

🕐 *PREP TIME: 5 MINUTES, COOK TIME: 6 HOURS, SERVES: 5*

🍸 **INGREDIENTS:**

- 5 ripe kiwis, peeled and sliced into ¼-inch rounds

😋 **DIRECTIONS:**

1. Arrange the kiwi slices in the air fry basket, making sure they don't overlap. Place the basket on the top rails of the oven.
2. Select DEHYDRATE, set the temperature to 135°F, and set the time to 6 hours. Close the oven door and press START/STOP to begin cooking.
3. Flip the kiwi slices halfway through the drying process.
4. Once dried, allow the kiwi chips to cool before storing or serving.

Cheesy Stuffed Mushrooms

🕐 **PREP TIME:** 15 MINUTES, **COOK TIME:** 12 MINUTES, **SERVES:** 4

🍷 INGREDIENTS:

- 16 large button mushrooms
- ½ cup shredded mozzarella cheese
- ⅓ cup grated Parmesan cheese
- 3 tbsps. chopped fresh parsley
- 1 clove garlic, minced
- Salt to taste

🍳 DIRECTIONS:

1. Clean and remove stems from the mushrooms.
2. In a bowl, mix mozzarella cheese, Parmesan cheese, parsley, garlic, and salt.
3. Stuff each mushroom cap with the cheese mixture.
4. Arrange the stuffed mushrooms in the air fry basket.
5. Select AIR FRY, set temperature to 375°F, and set time to 12 minutes. Press START/STOP to begin preheating.
6. When unit has preheated, place the basket on the top rails while sliding in the sheet pan and wire rack on the bottom rails to catch any cheese drips. Close oven door.
7. When cooking is complete, remove from the air fryer and let cool for a few minutes before serving.

• •

Spicy Zucchini Fries with Chipotle Ranch Dip

🕐 **PREP TIME:** 10 MINUTES, **COOK TIME:** 18 MINUTES, **SERVES:** 4-6

🍷 INGREDIENTS:

- Nonstick cooking spray
- 3 medium zucchinis, cut into ½-inch sticks
- 1 cup breadcrumbs
- ¼ cup grated Parmesan cheese
- 1 tsp. smoked paprika
- ½ tsp. cayenne pepper
- 1 egg, beaten

For the Chipotle Ranch Dip:
- ¼ cup ranch dressing
- 1 tbsp. chipotle hot sauce
- 1 tsp. lime juice

🍳 DIRECTIONS:

1. In a bowl, mix breadcrumbs, Parmesan cheese, smoked paprika, and cayenne pepper.
2. Dip zucchini sticks into the beaten egg, then coat them with the breadcrumb mixture.
3. Arrange zucchini fries in the air fry basket in a single layer and spray with nonstick cooking spray.
4. Select AIR FRY, set the temperature to 400°F, and set the time to 18 minutes. Press START/STOP to preheat.
5. Once preheated, place the basket on the top rails and close the oven door.
6. After 9 minutes, use tongs to flip the zucchini fries. Air fry for another 9 minutes until golden and crispy.
7. While the fries cook, mix ranch dressing, chipotle hot sauce, and lime juice to make the chipotle ranch dip.
8. When cooking is complete, serve the zucchini fries with the chipotle ranch dip.

Smoky Turkey Jerky

🕐 **PREP TIME:** 15 MINUTES, PLUS 3 HOURS MARINATING TIME, **COOK TIME:** 5 HOURS, **SERVES:** 4

🍴 INGREDIENTS:
- 1 lb. turkey breast, sliced thinly
- ¼ cup low-sodium soy sauce
- 2 tbsps. liquid smoke
- 1 tbsp. honey
- 1 tsp. black pepper
- 1 tsp. chili flakes (optional)

😋 DIRECTIONS:
1. Whisk together liquid smoke, soy sauce, honey, black pepper, and chili flakes in a bowl.
2. Add turkey slices to the marinade and refrigerate for 3 hours.
3. Arrange turkey slices in the air fry basket in a single layer. Place the basket on the top rails while sliding in the sheet pan and wire rack on the bottom rails.
4. Select DEHYDRATE, set temperature to 150°F, and set time to 5 hours. Close the oven door and press START/STOP to begin cooking.
5. Flip the turkey slices halfway through the cooking process.
6. When done, let the jerky cool before serving.

Crunchy Mozzarella Sticks with Marinara Dipping Sauce

🕐 **PREP TIME:** 5 MINUTES, **COOK TIME:** 12 MINUTES, **SERVES:** 4

🍴 INGREDIENTS:
- 1 box (22 oz.) frozen mozzarella sticks

For the Marinara Dipping Sauce:
- ½ cup marinara sauce
- 1 tsp. garlic powder
- 1 tsp. Italian seasoning
- 1 tbsp. grated Parmesan cheese

😋 DIRECTIONS:
1. Arrange the mozzarella sticks in the air fry basket in a single layer.
2. Select AIR FRY, set the temperature to 375°F, and set the time to 12 minutes. Press START/STOP to preheat.
3. Once preheated, place the basket on the top rails and close the oven door.
4. After 6 minutes, flip the mozzarella sticks and cook for another 6 minutes until golden and crispy.
5. While the sticks cook, heat the marinara sauce and stir in garlic powder, Italian seasoning, and Parmesan cheese.
6. When cooking is complete, serve the mozzarella sticks with warm marinara dipping sauce.

Dehydrated Strawberry Slices

🕐 **PREP TIME:** *5 MINUTES,* **COOK TIME:** *6 HOURS,* **SERVES:** *4*

🍷 INGREDIENTS:
- 2 cups fresh strawberries, hulled and sliced thinly

😋 DIRECTIONS:
1. Pat the strawberry slices dry with a paper towel to remove excess moisture.
2. Arrange the strawberry slices in the air fry basket in a single layer. Place the basket on the top rails.
3. Select DEHYDRATE, set the temperature to 135°F, and set the time to 6 hours. Close the oven door and press START/STOP to begin cooking.
4. Flip the strawberries halfway through to ensure even drying.
5. Once the strawberries are dry, allow them to cool before serving or storing.

Salmon Jerky

🕐 **PREP TIME:** *15 MINUTES, PLUS 1 HOUR MARINATING TIME,* **COOK TIME:** *4 HOURS,* **SERVES:** *6*

🍷 INGREDIENTS:
- 1½ lbs. fresh salmon fillet, skin removed, sliced thinly
- 2 tbsps. soy sauce
- 1 tbsp. maple syrup
- 1 tsp. garlic powder
- 1 tsp. smoked paprika
- ½ tsp. black pepper

😋 DIRECTIONS:
1. Mix soy sauce, maple syrup, garlic powder, smoked paprika, and black pepper in a bowl.
2. Marinate the salmon slices in the mixture for 1 hour in the refrigerator.
3. Arrange the salmon slices in the air fry basket without overlapping. Place the basket on the top rails while sliding in the sheet pan and wire rack on the bottom rails.
4. Select DEHYDRATE, set temperature to 150°F, and set time to 4 hours. Close the oven door and press START/STOP to begin cooking.
5. Flip the salmon slices halfway through the drying process.
6. Once dried, allow the salmon jerky to cool before serving.

Chocolate Chip Cookies

🕐 **PREP TIME:** *15 MINUTES,* **COOK TIME:** *12 MINUTES,* **SERVES:** *24 COOKIES*

🍽 INGREDIENTS:

- 1 cup (2 sticks) unsalted butter, softened
- ¾ cup granulated sugar
- ¾ cup packed brown sugar
- 1 large egg
- 2 tsps. vanilla extract
- 2¼ cups all-purpose flour
- 1 tsp. baking soda
- ½ tsp. baking powder
- ¼ tsp. salt
- 1 cup semisweet chocolate chips

👁 DIRECTIONS:

❶ In a large bowl, cream together the softened butter, granulated sugar, and brown sugar until light and fluffy. Beat in the egg and vanilla extract until well combined.

❷ In another bowl, whisk together the flour, baking soda, baking powder, and salt. Gradually add the dry ingredients to the wet mixture, mixing until just combined. Fold in the chocolate chips.

❸ Arrange rounded tablespoonfuls of cookie dough on the Ninja Sheet Pan, spaced 2 inches apart.

❹ Select BAKE, set temperature to 350°F, and set time to 12 minutes. Press START/STOP to begin preheating.

❺ When the unit has preheated, place the sheet pan on the wire rack on the bottom rails. Close the oven door.

❻ Bake until the edges are golden brown, about 12 minutes.

❼ When cooking is complete, let the cookies cool on the sheet pan for 5 minutes before transferring them to a wire rack to cool completely.

Homemade Vanilla Cake

🕐 **PREP TIME:** *20 MINUTES,* **COOK TIME:** *30 MINUTES,* **SERVES:** *8 SLICES*

🍽 INGREDIENTS:

- 1½ cups all-purpose flour
- 1 cup granulated sugar
- 2 large eggs
- 1 cup whole milk
- ½ cup unsalted butter, softened
- 2 tsps. baking powder
- 1 tsp. vanilla extract
- ¼ tsp. salt

👁 DIRECTIONS:

❶ Grease an 8-inch round baking pan and line the bottom with parchment paper.

❷ In a bowl, whisk together the flour, baking powder, and salt. In another large bowl, beat the softened butter and granulated sugar until creamy. Add eggs one at a time, beating well after each addition. Mix in the vanilla extract.

❸ Gradually add the flour mixture to the butter mixture alternately with the milk, beginning and ending with the flour mixture.

❹ Pour the batter into the prepared baking pan and smooth the top.

❺ Select BAKE, set temperature to 350°F, and set time to 30 minutes. Press START/STOP to begin preheating.

❻ When the unit has preheated, place the baking pan on the wire rack on the bottom rails. Close the oven door.

❼ Bake until a toothpick inserted into the center comes out clean, about 30 minutes.

❽ When cooking is complete, let the cake cool in the pan for 10 minutes, then transfer it to a wire rack to cool completely.

Lemon Bars

🕐 **PREP TIME:** *15 MINUTES*, **COOK TIME:** *30 MINUTES*, **SERVES:** *16 BARS*

🏆 INGREDIENTS:

For the Crust:
- 1 cup all-purpose flour
- ¼ cup granulated sugar
- ½ cup (1 stick) unsalted butter, chilled and cut into small pieces

For the Filling:
- 1 cup granulated sugar
- 2 tbsps. all-purpose flour
- 2 large eggs
- ⅓ cup freshly squeezed lemon juice
- 1 tsp. lemon zest

🍳 DIRECTIONS:

1. Grease an 8-inch square baking pan and line with parchment paper.
2. For the crust, in a bowl, combine flour and granulated sugar. Cut in the chilled butter until the mixture resembles coarse crumbs. Press the mixture evenly into the bottom of the prepared pan.
3. For the filling, in a bowl, whisk together granulated sugar and flour. Beat in eggs until smooth. Stir in lemon juice and zest until combined. Pour over the pre-baked crust.
4. Select BAKE, set temperature to 350°F, and set time to 30 minutes. Press START/STOP to begin preheating.
5. When the unit has preheated, place the baking pan on the wire rack on the bottom rails. Close the oven door.
6. Bake until the filling is set and the edges are lightly golden, about 30 minutes.
7. When cooking is complete, let cool completely in the pan before cutting into bars.

Vanilla Pumpkin Bread

🕐 **PREP TIME:** *15 MINUTES*, **COOK TIME:** *50 MINUTES*, **SERVES:** *10 SLICES*

🏆 INGREDIENTS:

- 1¾ cups all-purpose flour
- 1 tsp. baking soda
- ½ tsp. baking powder
- ½ tsp. salt
- 1 tsp. ground cinnamon
- ¼ tsp. ground nutmeg
- ¼ tsp. ground cloves
- 1 cup granulated sugar
- ½ cup packed brown sugar
- ½ cup vegetable oil
- 1 cup canned pumpkin puree
- 2 large eggs
- 1 tsp. vanilla extract

🍳 DIRECTIONS:

1. Grease a 9x5-inch loaf pan.
2. In a bowl, whisk together the flour, baking soda, baking powder, salt, cinnamon, nutmeg, and cloves.
3. In another bowl, mix the granulated sugar, brown sugar, vegetable oil, pumpkin puree, eggs, and vanilla extract until well combined.
4. Gradually add the dry ingredients to the wet mixture, stirring until just combined.
5. Pour the batter into the prepared loaf pan and smooth the top.
6. Select BAKE, set temperature to 350°F, and set time to 50 minutes. Press START/STOP to begin preheating.
7. When the unit has preheated, place the loaf pan on the wire rack on the bottom rails. Close the oven door.
8. Bake until a toothpick inserted into the center comes out clean, about 50 minutes.
9. When cooking is complete, let the bread cool in the pan for 10 minutes, then transfer to a wire rack to cool completely.

Best Pecan Pie

⏱ **PREP TIME:** 20 MINUTES, PLUS 30 MINUTES REFRIGERATING TIME, **COOK TIME:** 50 MINUTES, **SERVES:** 8 SLICES

🍸 INGREDIENTS:

For the Crust:
- 1½ cups all-purpose flour
- ¼ tsp. salt
- ½ cup (1 stick) unsalted butter, cold and cut into small pieces
- 3-4 tbsps. ice water

For the Filling:
- 1 cup light corn syrup
- 1 cup packed brown sugar
- ¼ cup unsalted butter, melted
- 3 large eggs
- 1¼ cups pecan halves
- 1 tsp. vanilla extract

😋 DIRECTIONS:

1. For the crust, in a bowl, mix flour and salt. Cut in the cold butter until the mixture resembles coarse crumbs. Stir in ice water, a tablespoon at a time, until the dough comes together. Press the dough into a 9-inch pie pan. Refrigerate for 30 minutes.
2. For the filling, in a large bowl, whisk together corn syrup, brown sugar, melted butter, eggs, and vanilla extract. Stir in the pecan halves.
3. Pour the filling into the chilled pie crust.
4. Select BAKE, set temperature to 375°F, and set time to 50 minutes. Press START/STOP to begin preheating.
5. When the unit has preheated, place the pie on the wire rack on the bottom rails. Close the oven door.
6. Bake until the filling is set and the crust is golden brown, about 50 minutes.
7. When cooking is complete, let the pie cool before serving.

Chocolate Lava Cake

⏱ **PREP TIME:** 15 MINUTES, **COOK TIME:** 12 MINUTES, **SERVES:** 4 CAKES

🍸 INGREDIENTS:
- ½ cup (1 stick) unsalted butter
- 1 cup semi-sweet chocolate chips
- 1 cup powdered sugar
- 2 large eggs
- 2 large egg yolks
- 1 tsp. vanilla extract
- ½ cup all-purpose flour
- Pinch of salt
- Butter and cocoa powder, for greasing ramekins

😋 DIRECTIONS:

1. Grease four 6-ounce ramekins with butter and dust with cocoa powder, tapping out excess.
2. In a medium bowl, melt the butter and chocolate chips together in the microwave in 30-second intervals, stirring until smooth.
3. Stir in the powdered sugar until combined. Add the eggs, egg yolks, and vanilla extract, mixing until well combined. Gently fold in the flour and salt.
4. Divide the batter evenly among the prepared ramekins.
5. Select BAKE, set temperature to 425°F, and set time to 12 minutes. Press START/STOP to begin preheating.
6. When the unit has preheated, place the ramekins on the wire rack on the bottom rails. Close the oven door.
7. Bake until the edges are set but the centers are soft, about 12 minutes.
8. When cooking is complete, let the cakes cool in the ramekins for 1 minute. Run a knife around the edges to loosen and invert onto plates. Serve immediately.

Walnut Brownies

🕐 **PREP TIME:** *15 MINUTES,* **COOK TIME:** *25 MINUTES,* **SERVES:** *16*

🍸 INGREDIENTS:

- ½ cup (1 stick) unsalted butter
- 1 cup granulated sugar
- 2 large eggs
- 1 tsp. vanilla extract
- ½ cup unsweetened cocoa powder
- 1 cup all-purpose flour
- ¼ tsp. baking powder
- ¼ tsp. salt
- 1 cup chopped walnuts

🍮 DIRECTIONS:

1. Grease a 9x9-inch baking pan.
2. In a medium saucepan, melt the butter over medium heat. Remove from heat and stir in granulated sugar, eggs, and vanilla extract.
3. Mix in the cocoa powder, flour, baking powder, and salt until just combined. Fold in the chopped walnuts.
4. Pour the batter into the prepared baking pan and spread evenly.
5. Select BAKE, set temperature to 350°F, and set time to 25 minutes. Press START/STOP to begin preheating.
6. When the unit has preheated, place the baking pan on the wire rack on the bottom rails. Close the oven door.
7. Bake until a toothpick inserted into the center comes out with a few moist crumbs, about 25 minutes.
8. When cooking is complete, let the brownies cool in the pan before cutting into squares.

Apple Crisp

🕐 **PREP TIME:** *15 MINUTES,* **COOK TIME:** *45 MINUTES,* **SERVES:** *6*

🍸 INGREDIENTS:

For the Filling:
- 6 cups peeled, cored, and sliced apples (about 6 medium apples)
- ¼ cup granulated sugar
- ¼ cup packed brown sugar
- 1 tsp. ground cinnamon
- ¼ tsp. ground nutmeg
- 1 tbsp. lemon juice

For the Topping:
- ½ cup all-purpose flour
- ½ cup rolled oats
- ¼ cup granulated sugar
- ¼ cup packed brown sugar
- ¼ tsp. ground cinnamon
- ¼ cup (½ stick) unsalted butter, cold and cut into small pieces

🍮 DIRECTIONS:

1. In a large bowl, toss the apple slices with granulated sugar, brown sugar, cinnamon, nutmeg, and lemon juice. Transfer the apple mixture to a greased 8x8-inch baking dish.
2. For the topping, in a bowl, mix flour, oats, granulated sugar, brown sugar, and cinnamon. Cut in the cold butter until the mixture resembles coarse crumbs. Sprinkle the topping evenly over the apples.
3. Select BAKE, set temperature to 350°F, and set time to 45 minutes. Press START/STOP to begin preheating.
4. When the unit has preheated, place the baking dish on the wire rack on the bottom rails. Close the oven door.
5. Bake until the topping is golden brown and the apples are tender, about 45 minutes.
6. When cooking is complete, let the apple crisp cool slightly before serving.

Cinnamon Rolls

🕐 **PREP TIME:** 20 MINUTES, **COOK TIME:** 20 MINUTES, **SERVES:** 12 ROLLS

🍷 INGREDIENTS:

For the Dough:
- 2¼ cups all-purpose flour
- ¼ cup granulated sugar
- 2 tsps. baking powder
- ¼ tsp. salt
- ½ cup (1 stick) unsalted butter, cold and cut into small pieces
- ¾ cup milk

For the Filling:
- ¼ cup unsalted butter, softened
- ½ cup brown sugar
- 2 tbsps. ground cinnamon

For the Icing:
- 1 cup powdered sugar
- 2 tbsps. milk
- 1 tsp. vanilla extract

😋 DIRECTIONS:

1. For the dough, in a bowl, whisk together flour, granulated sugar, baking powder, and salt. Cut in the cold butter until the mixture resembles coarse crumbs. Stir in the milk until a dough forms. Roll out the dough on a floured surface into a rectangle.
2. For the filling, spread the softened butter over the dough. Sprinkle with brown sugar and cinnamon. Roll the dough tightly and cut into 12 equal slices. Arrange the rolls in a greased baking dish.
3. Select BAKE, set temperature to 375°F, and set time to 20 minutes. Press START/STOP to begin preheating.
4. When the unit has preheated, place the baking dish on the wire rack on the bottom rails. Close the oven door.
5. Bake until the rolls are golden brown, about 20 minutes.
6. When cooking is complete, mix together the powdered sugar, milk, and vanilla extract for the icing. Drizzle over the warm rolls before serving.

Peanut Butter Cookies

🕐 **PREP TIME:** 15 MINUTES, **COOK TIME:** 10 MINUTES, **SERVES:** 24 COOKIES

🍷 INGREDIENTS:

- ½ cup (1 stick) unsalted butter, softened
- ½ cup peanut butter
- ½ cup granulated sugar
- ½ cup packed brown sugar
- 1 large egg
- 1 tsp. vanilla extract
- 1¼ cups all-purpose flour
- 1 tsp. baking soda
- ¼ tsp. salt

😋 DIRECTIONS:

1. In a large bowl, cream together the softened butter, peanut butter, granulated sugar, and brown sugar until smooth. Beat in the egg and vanilla extract until well combined.
2. In another bowl, whisk together the flour, baking soda, and salt. Gradually add the dry ingredients to the wet mixture, mixing until just combined.
3. Roll tablespoonfuls of dough into balls and place them on the Ninja Sheet Pan, spacing them 2 inches apart. Flatten each ball with a fork, making a crisscross pattern.
4. Select BAKE, set temperature to 350°F, and set time to 10 minutes. Press START/STOP to begin preheating.
5. When the unit has preheated, place the sheet pan on the wire rack on the bottom rails. Close the oven door.
6. Bake until the edges are lightly golden, about 10 minutes.
7. When cooking is complete, let the cookies cool on the sheet pan for 5 minutes before transferring them to a wire rack to cool completely.

Classic Blueberry Muffins

🕐 **PREP TIME:** 15 MINUTES, **COOK TIME:** 25 MINUTES, **SERVES:** 12 MUFFINS

🍸 INGREDIENTS:

- 1½ cups all-purpose flour
- ½ cup granulated sugar
- ½ cup packed brown sugar
- ½ cup unsalted butter, melted
- 2 large eggs
- 1 cup milk
- 1 tsp. vanilla extract
- 2 tsps. baking powder
- ¼ tsp. salt
- 1 cup fresh blueberries (or frozen, if preferred)

🍴 DIRECTIONS:

① Line a 12-cup muffin tin with paper liners.
② In a bowl, whisk together the flour, granulated sugar, brown sugar, baking powder, and salt.
③ In another bowl, mix the melted butter, eggs, milk, and vanilla extract.
④ Gradually add the wet ingredients to the dry ingredients, mixing until just combined. Gently fold in the blueberries.
⑤ Divide the batter evenly among the muffin cups.
⑥ Select BAKE, set temperature to 375°F, and set time to 25 minutes. Press START/STOP to begin preheating.
⑦ When the unit has preheated, place the muffin tin on the wire rack on the bottom rails. Close the oven door.
⑧ Bake until a toothpick inserted into the center of a muffin comes out clean, about 25 minutes.
⑨ When cooking is complete, let the muffins cool in the tin for 5 minutes before transferring them to a wire rack to cool completely.

Raspberry Almond Tart

🕐 **PREP TIME:** 20 MINUTES, **COOK TIME:** 40 MINUTES, **SERVES:** 8

🍸 INGREDIENTS:

For the Crust:
- 1 cup all-purpose flour
- ¼ cup granulated sugar
- ¼ tsp. salt
- ½ cup (1 stick) unsalted butter, cold and cut into small pieces

For the Filling:
- ½ cup almond meal
- ½ cup granulated sugar
- ¼ cup unsalted butter, softened
- 1 large egg
- ¼ tsp. almond extract
- ⅓ cup raspberry jam

🍴 DIRECTIONS:

① In a bowl, mix flour, granulated sugar, and salt. Cut in cold butter until the mixture resembles coarse crumbs. Press mixture into the bottom and up the sides of a tart pan.
② Select BAKE, set temperature to 350°F, and set time to 15 minutes. Press START/STOP to begin preheating.
③ When the unit has preheated, place the tart pan on the wire rack on the bottom rails. Close the oven door.
④ Bake until the crust is golden, about 15 minutes. Let cool slightly.
⑤ For the filling, in a bowl, cream together almond meal, granulated sugar, and softened butter. Beat in egg and almond extract. Spread the filling evenly over the pre-baked crust.
⑥ Drop spoonfuls of raspberry jam over the almond filling and swirl gently with a knife.
⑦ Continue baking until the filling is set and golden, about 25 minutes.
⑧ When cooking is complete, let cool completely before slicing.

Almond Biscotti

🕐 **PREP TIME:** 20 MINUTES, **COOK TIME:** 35 MINUTES, **SERVES:** 24 BISCOTTI

🍸 INGREDIENTS:

- 2 cups all-purpose flour
- 1 cup granulated sugar
- 1 tsp. baking powder
- ¼ tsp. salt
- ¼ cup unsalted butter, melted
- 2 large eggs
- 1 tsp. vanilla extract
- 1 cup whole almonds, toasted and chopped

🍳 DIRECTIONS:

1. Line a baking sheet with parchment paper.
2. In a large bowl, whisk together flour, sugar, baking powder, and salt. In another bowl, combine melted butter, eggs, and vanilla extract.
3. Mix wet ingredients into dry ingredients until just combined. Fold in the almonds.
4. Shape the dough into a 12-inch log on the prepared baking sheet.
5. Select BAKE, set temperature to 350°F, and set time to 35 minutes. Press START/STOP to begin preheating.
6. When the unit has preheated, place the baking sheet on the wire rack on the bottom rails. Close the oven door.
7. Bake until the log is golden brown, about 35 minutes. Remove from the oven and let cool for 10 minutes. Slice into ½-inch thick pieces.
8. Return the slices to the baking sheet and bake for an additional 10 minutes, flipping halfway through, until crisp.
9. When cooking is complete, let the biscotti cool completely.

Coconut Macaroons

🕐 **PREP TIME:** 15 MINUTES, **COOK TIME:** 20 MINUTES, **SERVES:** 24 MACAROONS

🍸 INGREDIENTS:

- 2⅓ cups sweetened shredded coconut
- ½ cup granulated sugar
- ¼ cup all-purpose flour
- ⅛ tsp. salt
- 3 large egg whites
- 1 tsp. vanilla extract
- ¼ cup semi-sweet chocolate chips (optional, for drizzling)

🍳 DIRECTIONS:

1. Line a baking sheet with parchment paper. In a bowl, mix shredded coconut, granulated sugar, flour, and salt.
2. In another bowl, beat egg whites and vanilla extract until stiff peaks form. Gently fold the egg whites into the coconut mixture until well combined.
3. Drop rounded tablespoons of the mixture onto the prepared baking sheet.
4. Select BAKE, set temperature to 325°F, and set time to 20 minutes. Press START/STOP to begin preheating.
5. When the unit has preheated, place the baking sheet on the wire rack on the bottom rails. Close the oven door.
6. Bake until the macaroons are golden brown, about 20 minutes.
7. When cooking is complete, let cool completely. If desired, melt chocolate chips and drizzle over cooled macaroons.

Appendix 1:
Basic Kitchen Conversions & Equivalents

DRY MEASUREMENTS CONVERSION CHART

3 teaspoons = 1 tablespoon = 1/16 cup
6 teaspoons = 2 tablespoons = 1/8 cup
12 teaspoons = 4 tablespoons = ¼ cup
24 teaspoons = 8 tablespoons = ½ cup
36 teaspoons = 12 tablespoons = ¾ cup
48 teaspoons = 16 tablespoons = 1 cup

METRIC TO US COOKING CONVERSIONS

OVEN TEMPERATURES

120 °C = 250 °F
160 °C = 320 °F
180 °C = 350 °F
205 °C = 400 °F
220 °C = 425 °F

LIQUID MEASUREMENTS CONVERSION CHART

8 fluid ounces = 1 cup = ½ pint = ¼ quart
16 fluid ounces = 2 cups = 1 pint = ½ quart
32 fluid ounces = 4 cups = 2 pints = 1 quart = ¼ gallon
128 fluid ounces = 16 cups = 8 pints = 4 quarts = 1 gallon

BAKING IN GRAMS

1 cup flour = 140 grams
1 cup sugar = 150 grams
1 cup powdered sugar = 160 grams
1 cup heavy cream = 235 grams

VOLUME

1 milliliter = 1/5 teaspoon
5 ml = 1 teaspoon
15 ml = 1 tablespoon
240 ml = 1 cup or 8 fluid ounces
1 liter = 34 fluid ounces

WEIGHT

1 gram = .035 ounces
100 grams = 3.5 ounces
500 grams = 1.1 pounds
1 kilogram = 35 ounces

US TO METRIC COOKING CONVERSIONS

1/5 tsp = 1 ml
1 tsp = 5 ml
1 tbsp = 15 ml
1 fluid ounces = 30 ml
1 cup = 237 ml
1 pint (2 cups) = 473 ml
1 quart (4 cups) = .95 liter
1 gallon (16 cups) = 3.8 liters
1 oz = 28 grams
1 pound = 454 grams

BUTTER

1 cup butter = 2 sticks = 8 ounces = 230 grams = 16 tablespoons

WHAT DOES 1 CUP EQUAL

1 cup = 8 fluid ounces
1 cup = 16 tablespoons
1 cup = 48 teaspoons
1 cup = ½ pint
1 cup = ¼ quart
1 cup = 1/16 gallon
1 cup = 240 ml

BAKING PAN CONVERSIONS

9-inch round cake pan = 12 cups
10-inch tube pan =16 cups
10-inch bundt pan = 12 cups
9-inch springform pan = 10 cups
9 x 5 inch loaf pan = 8 cups
9-inch square pan = 8 cups

BAKING PAN CONVERSIONS

1 cup all-purpose flour = 4.5 oz
1 cup rolled oats = 3 oz
1 large egg = 1.7 oz
1 cup butter = 8 oz
1 cup milk = 8 oz
1 cup heavy cream = 8.4 oz
1 cup granulated sugar = 7.1 oz
1 cup packed brown sugar = 7.75 oz
1 cup vegetable oil = 7.7 oz
1 cup unsifted powdered sugar = 4.4 oz

Appendix 2:
Ninja Air Fry Cooking Chart

Ingredient	Amount	Preparation	Oil	Temp	Cook Time
Frozen Food					
Chicken nuggets	2 boxes (12 oz each)	None	None	400°F	20-25 mins
Crab cakes	6 cakes (3 oz each)	None	Brush with oil	390°F	15-20 mins
Fish fillets (breaded)	1 package (10 fillets)	None	None	400°F	15-20 mins
Fish sticks	1 bag (24.5 oz)	None	None	400°F	15-20 mins
French fries	1 bag (32 oz)	None	None	390°F	25-30 mins
Mozzarella sticks	1 box (22 oz)	None	None	375°F	10-15 mins
Pizza rolls	1 bag (24.8 oz, 50 count)	None	None	375°F	10-15 mins
Popcorn shrimp	2 boxes (14 oz each)	None	None	390°F	15-20 mins
Pot stickers	2 bags (16 oz each)	None	1 Tbsp	390°F	15-20 mins
Sweet potato fries	1 bag (20 oz)	None	None	375°F	25-30 mins
Tater tots	1 bag (32 oz)	None	None	360°F	20-25 mins
Meat, Poultry, Fish					
Bacon	½ package (8 oz)	None	None	390°F	10-15 mins
Burgers (80% lean)	4-6 burgers (¼-lb each)	1 inch thick	None	375°F	15-20 mins
Chicken drumsticks	6 drumsticks	Pat dry	Brush with oil	400°F	25-35 mins
Chicken thighs (bone-in, skin-on)	4 thighs (6-8 oz each)	Pat dry	Brush with oil	390°F	20-25 mins
Chicken wings	2-2½ lbs	Pat dry	1 Tbsp	400°F	25-35 mins
Salmon fillets	5 fillets (6-8 oz each)	None	Brush with oil	390°F	15-20 mins
Sausage	12 sausages, whole (approx. 2 lbs)	None	None	390°F	15-20 mins
Shrimp	2 lbs Large fresh or frozen, thawed. Peeled, deveined	None	None	390°F	5-10 mins

Vegetables					
Asparagus	2 bunches (16 oz each)	Cut in half, ends trimmed	2 Tbsp	420°F	10-15 mins
Bell peppers	3-4 medium peppers	Seeded, cut in quarters	1 Tbsp	400°F	15-20 mins
Broccoli	1-2 large heads	Cut in 1-2-inch florets	1 Tbsp	400°F	10-15 mins
Brussels sprouts	1-2 lbs	Cut in half, remove stems	1 Tbsp	400°F	10-15 mins
Carrots	1 lb	Peeled, cut in ¼-inch rounds	1 Tbsp	425°F	10-15 mins
Cauliflower	1 head	Cut in 1-2-inch florets	2 Tbsp	400°F	15-20 mins
Corn on the cob	4-6 ears	Whole ears, remove husks	1 Tbsp	400°F	25-30 mins
Green beans	1 bag (12 oz)	Trim	1 Tbsp	400°F	10-15 mins
Kale	4 cups, packed (4 oz)	Tear into pieces, remove stems	1 Tbsp	325°F	5-10 mins
Mushrooms	16 oz	Rinsed, sliced ¼-inch thick	1 Tbsp	390°F	10-15 mins
Potatoes, russet (wedges)	1½ lbs	Cut in 1-inch wedges	1 Tbsp	390°F	25-30 mins
Potatoes, russet (fries)	1 lb	Hand-cut fries, ¼-inch thick, soak 30 mins in cold water, pat dry	1-2 Tbsp	400°F	20-25 mins
Potatoes, sweet	1 lb	Hand-cut fries, ¼-inch thick, soak 30 mins in cold water, pat dry	1 Tbsp	375°F	25-30 mins
Zucchini	1 lb (3 medium)	Cut in half lengthwise, then cut in ½-in pieces	1 Tbsp	400°F	15-20 mins

Appendix 3: Recipes Index

Made in United States
Troutdale, OR
11/24/2024

25264528R00042